CATHY NEWMAN is the first female main presenter of Channel 4 News and the bestselling author of *Bloody Brilliant Women*. She spent over a decade on Fleet Street, latterly with the *Financial Times*. Since joining Channel 4 News in 2006 she has broadcast a string of scoops, including allegations of violent abuse against the British barrister John Smyth, sexual harassment allegations against the Liberal Democrat peer Lord Rennard, and an investigation into a British sex offender, Simon Harris, which saw him jailed for 17 years. In April 2020 she was named as one of the launch presenters for the new Times Radio station, presenting the Friday drive time show. And in 2022, she added the role of Investigations Editor to her Channel 4 brief. Cathy has also written for the *Independent* and the *Daily Telegraph*. She is married to John O'Connell, a writer, and they have two children.

T0337474

THE LADDER

*Life Lessons from Women Who Scaled
the Heights & Dodged the Snakes*

Cathy Newman

WILLIAM
COLLINS

William Collins
An imprint of HarperCollins*Publishers*
1 London Bridge Street
London SE1 9GF

WilliamCollinsBooks.com

HarperCollins*Publishers*
Macken House
39/40 Mayor Street Upper
Dublin 1
D01 C9W8, Ireland

First published in Great Britain in 2024 by William Collins
This William Collins paperback edition published in 2025

1

Set in Sabon LT Std by HarperCollins*Publishers* India

Printed and bound in the UK using 100% Renewable
Electricity at CPI Group (UK) Ltd

This book contains FSC™ certified paper and other controlled
sources to ensure responsible forest management.

For more information visit: www.harpercollins.co.uk/green

CONTENTS

INTRODUCTION

It's lucky I like to chat, otherwise I don't know how I'd get through three hours of live radio. Any other day of the week, I'm likely to be found anchoring *Channel 4 News*. But on Friday afternoons I present the drivetime show on Times Radio, serving up a smorgasbord of stories, voices and viewpoints – from whale noises and interviews with supermodels to serious political news.

One of my favourite segments, intended to conclude the show on a thoughtful, upbeat note, is called *The Ladder*. It lasts half an hour and sees me interviewing a trailblazing woman who has achieved something extraordinary in her field. Usually that field is professional, but talk often turns to the personal; to the interplay between those two spheres and the effort it takes, as a woman, to make them function in tandem. On many occasions I've thought: these stories are so inspiring, they'd make a great book. And lo, it came to pass!

The core of this book version of *The Ladder* is the same as it is on the radio: wise advice from one woman to another. It draws on and is inspired by interviews conducted by me for the show, and augmented by other resources where appropriate, to take readers on a journey through some of the most urgent issues facing women today – the challenges of growing, working, loving and ageing.

My producers and I called the slot *The Ladder* because we anticipated it being about progress and ascent, and so it has been. But the interviews have been so wide-ranging, not to say different in tone, that I've realised the title doesn't always do them justice. Well, it does – but only if you accept that a ladder doesn't have to go straight up: that it can be at a slant or a zig-zag, or like an Escher staircase where it isn't easy to tell what is up and what is down or where the steps are leading.

For what becomes clear after listening to the interviews is that women's progress never follows a simple, linear trajectory but has always been marked by periods of advancement, setback and struggle. Progress in one area does not translate into progress in other spheres. While there have been significant advancements, gender inequality remains rife across the world. We in the West dwell, justifiably, on issues like the gender pay gap. In Africa, the biggest problem is gender-based violence, described by the United Nations as 'the most widespread but least visible human rights violation in the world'. (In 2021, UN Women Executive Director Phumzile Mlambo-Ngcuka talked of how the multiple impacts of Covid-19 had triggered a 'shadow pandemic' of increased reported violence of all kinds against women and girls.[1])

Women's progress is a complex, evolving journey, then; one marked by collective effort, policy change and broad social movements as well as individual achievements.

I still like the idea of a wonky, makeshift ladder, though. So what might be at the top of it? I'd say fulfilment, in the broadest sense. That encompasses happiness; personal safety; balance; positive relationships; good health; self-knowledge; a sense of purpose; and, last but not least, professional success, which is often a more complex, double-edged proposition for women than it is for men, who don't have to worry about glass ceilings and pay gaps. It can pull those other elements together or throw them out of balance – and some of the most interesting tales address this tension directly.

Way back in 1994, shortly after I left university, the late Kate Figes wrote about the way we (i.e. women) 'look to the few women who do hold positions of influence as guiding lights. We expect them to change the culture they find themselves in, to kick down centuries of discriminatory practice and to feel automatic empathy for other women's secondary status, simply because of their gender.'[2]

This remains the case, notwithstanding the emergence in the last decade of a whole culture based around sometimes spurious 'influencing'. But while Figes seemed troubled by the burden our expectation places on those 'guiding light' women, I haven't sensed any reluctance or hesitation in the ones who have spoken to me for *The Ladder*. I suspect they feel as I do, that only good can come from sharing knowledge and experiences. As the deaf-blind American political activist Helen Keller famously put it: 'Knowledge is love and light and vision.'

I like hearing women talk about their lives because, growing up in suburban Surrey, I heard men's stories often but women's only rarely. My father taught chemistry at a public school to which girls were only admitted in the sixth form. It was a traditional, male world. When, back in 1993, Prime Minister John Major channelled George Orwell to invoke a Britain characterised by 'long shadows on county cricket grounds', 'warm beer', 'dog lovers' and 'old maids bicycling to Holy Communion through the morning mist', I thought: *Yep, sounds familiar.*

Don't get me wrong, I had a loving, lucky, privileged childhood. Both my parents were teachers with university educations. But few of the women I knew when I was a child chose to analyse their lives in a way that would have revealed fault lines, complications or injustices (both suffered and perpetuated). To do so would have been seen as 'self-indulgent'.

The early-1970s fashion for 'consciousness-raising' – discussing the private, subjective experience of being a woman – passed my mother's earlier generation by. They regarded it as faddish and unhelpful, just as minority groups at the time saw it as a predominantly white 'leisure-class' practice.

Ironically, considering what I do for a living, my family didn't get a telly until I was 16. Only then did I see Kate Adie reporting from far-flung, war-torn places and realise women could do journalism too.

All of that has changed. Now, a mighty wave of women – and not just the straight, white ones who arguably got the most out of second-wave feminism – have found their voices online, in blogs, in podcasts. Slowly, society is accepting that even the word 'woman' contains multitudes. 'There is no such thing as a "pure" experience of womanhood,' writes Hilary M Lips in her book *Women Across Cultures*. 'Factors such as race, ethnicity, class, culture, nationality, age, sexual orientation, gender identity and ability intertwine with gender, such that what it means and how it feels to be a woman is different in various combinations of these dimensions.'[3] These strike me as wise words and I've tried to bear them in mind in what follows.

These days we still talk about what it means to be a woman. But sometimes we do it so loudly and angrily, and from within such different ideological silos, it's as if we're behaving not like people so much as brands that need promoting; as if the only point of communication is to secure clicks and likes and shares – to survive and prosper in a buzzing marketplace of personalities. This is a shame because in an age of anxiety like the one we're currently living through, listening to other women's stories is, or should be, hugely consoling. Even when someone is describing an emotion you've never felt or an experience you've never had, it's instructive to ask yourself: *Who am I in this story?* The answer is not always obvious and often comes as something of a surprise.

I'm used to doing tough interviews with slippery politicians. But *The Ladder* requires something different from me, to the point where sometimes I feel more like an analyst than a journalist. Rather than frowny finger-wagging, there's a calm, non-judgemental teasing out of revelations. I must admit I find the change in style refreshing, and I always come away inspired and humbled.

Offering inspiration and wise counsel are some of the world's most acclaimed and influential women, from politicians like Angela Rayner and lawyers like Brenda Hale to scientists such as Dame Jocelyn Bell Burnell, activists like Rosamund Adoo-Kissi-Debrah, film-makers like Waad Al-Kateab, religious leaders like Rose Hudson-Wilkin, actors like Juliet Stevenson and Maureen Lipman and fellow broadcasters like Joan Bakewell, Clare Balding and Davina McCall. I'd like to thank them all for being so generous with their time.

Often, the women I speak to have discovered some unexpected resource within themselves. Perhaps as a result of illness or other adversity, they have reimagined what it means to be happy, healthy and successful. Former union leader Rehana Azam endured and then escaped from an abusive forced marriage arranged by her parents, while Baroness Arminka Helić became a foreign policy expert after fleeing the Yugoslav conflict in the 1990s by crossing a river on a raft.

Key questions arise throughout our lifetimes. How much are we the products of our childhoods? When does confidence become overconfidence? How can we understand each other better? Is changing your mind a sign of strength or weakness?

Do we still have the patience to listen and the time to understand? Are we attentive not just to the words people utter but, as the psychoanalyst Stephen Grosz puts it, 'the gaps in between'? Are the goals women have traditionally set themselves still meaningful?

In attempting to answer these questions this book will, I hope, go some way towards unlocking the spiritual and psychological potential of the complex lives we live today.

Of course, it's not so long – only one hundred and fifty years – since middle- and upper-class ladies were discouraged from climbing any ladders at all,[4] even wooden ones in their own homes; though no one minded if working-class women found themselves in physical danger in factories, in domestic service or through having endless children.

Nowadays successful women hail from every social class and are no longer seen as deviant and iconoclastic. We take for granted that women can be judges, doctors and lawyers – anything they want! But it does sometimes feel like an agreement that has been bashed out in a hurry with little regard for how it will work in practice.

Is it a surprise that so many women in senior leadership positions are bailing out? McKinsey's 2022 Women in the Workplace report was based on a survey of 40,000 diverse women across 333 participating US companies. Its findings made for stark reading:

'Women leaders are just as ambitious as men, but at many companies, they face headwinds that signal it will be harder to advance. They're more likely to experience belittling microaggressions, such as having their judgement questioned or being mistaken for someone more junior. They're doing more to support employee well-being and foster inclusion, but this critical work is spreading them thin and going mostly unrewarded.

And finally, it's increasingly important to women leaders that they work for companies that prioritise flexibility, employee well-being, and diversity, equity, and inclusion (DEI).'[5]

Since their grudging admittance to the top table – or any tables at all – women have known that work can never be the only thing in life. They've known this because they were usually the ones combining work with cooking, cleaning and caring for children and/or elderly relatives.

It's true that many more men are involved on this front than was the case even twenty years ago. Still, a 2020 YouGov survey found that, while men were very good at gardening and putting the bins out, they remained useless at food shopping and washing up.[6] And when they do rise to the challenge, they are applauded for it to a degree that feels frankly surreal – hailed as 'new men', 'hands-on dads', etc.

I'm trying to explain, I suppose, why women's stories are more interesting to me than most men's. Ultimately it's because of the way society still indulges men and cushions them from the full impact of failure. Men's journey up the ladder is smoother and more predictable than women's because they never doubt their right to climb it.

It's telling, I think, that former Prime Minister Tony Blair claimed never to have come across the term 'imposter syndrome'[7] whereas *every* woman knows the phenomenon, which I discuss at length in Chapter 2.

It stands to reason that, on your way up any ladder, you're going to find rungs that are broken. Sometimes, when we reach those rungs, we will slip down and when that happens we will panic. The trick is to put those moments of uncertainty and fear to productive use; to accept that, although what we're climbing through is thin air, we're still going somewhere valuable.

Let me give an example from my own life. Before I joined *Channel 4 News* in 2006 I had never done what's known in the trade as a 'two-way' – a live outside-broadcast interview conducted by an anchor-presenter safely ensconced in a studio. For my first ever two-way as Political Correspondent, I had to stand outside Liberal Democrat Party HQ in Westminster and make some meaningful contribution to the story of the day, whatever that was. But all I could think about was how scared I was and how sleep-deprived from all the weeks of anticipatory worrying.

It was in the winter so it was dark. The harsh lights made my eyes water. I could feel my heart beating in great rhythmic surges as I was cued in and Jon Snow asked, 'So Cathy, what's been going on there?'

In a clipped, tense voice I started to answer. I was concentrating so intently on not gabbling, not saying 'er' and not repeatedly looking down at my notes that I failed to notice I was standing in the middle of the road.

In fact, I only fully comprehended this when the lights of a fast-approaching taxi flared on the damp asphalt. If it maintained its current speed it would hit me in, oh, five seconds?

A single choice presented itself: move and save my life or carry on talking and save my career, assuming I still had one.

I opted to carry on talking.

The taxi saw me just in time and came to a halt.

'Well Cathy,' said Jon's voice, 'that all sounds very interesting . . .'

I went home that night convinced I'd failed, that I wasn't cut out for TV. But no one seemed to have noticed what a disaster it was. Praise isn't generally forthcoming in the world of TV news. Instead, the standard response to not screwing something up is silence and indifference – and there was plenty of that, so it can't have been terrible.

My parents seemed to think it had gone well. Ditto my husband, who had recorded it. He and I watched it later, scrutinising my performance with furrow-browed intensity.

'I look,' I said, 'like a rabbit having a panic attack.'

'But in a good way,' said my husband. 'And only for a second.'

Gradually, over the course of many months, I got less scared until now it feels weirdly normal to be broadcasting to the nation. More normal than cooking dinner, at any rate.

I had learned, right at the start of my TV career, that it was possible for things to go wrong. That time I got away with it, but in future I might not be so lucky.

And indeed plenty more did go wrong. There was the time I lost my way in a live two-way about sex offenders and found myself repeating the words 'sex offenders' and 'sex offences' for what felt like an eternity until I found my way out of the verbal maze I'd mistakenly entered. Or the time very early in my presenting career when the autocue broke and I forgot

I had the paper scripts somewhere to hand. I found myself looking from one camera to another, heart racing, voice trembling, while the programme editor yelled unhelpfully in my ear.

The psychoanalyst Irvin Yalom wrote a wonderful book called *Love's Executioner and Other Tales of Psychotherapy* which comprised a selection of case studies from his professional practice. I'll be mentioning it again later, I'm sure, but for now one story stands out for me. It concerns a woman called Eva, who one day had her purse stolen and was completely undone by it, not because of the money she lost but because she had always thought of herself as the kind of person to whom bad things didn't happen. That is to say, she had a deep belief in her own specialness, her inviolability – something most of us have as children until it is taken away from us, either through experience over time or, in some tragic cases, prematurely, by other darker means.

Recognising that bad things will happen to us and that that is part of life is one of the most important lessons of all. It's one I remember every time I'm out in London and I see a black cab hurtling towards me with its lights glaring . . .

Over the past decade technology has transformed the workplace: a revolution catalysed in the last couple of years by the pandemic. As a result women have changed the way they conceive and structure their lives. They've had to embrace flux and rethink basic concepts to do with home, work, love, commitment and children. For many of us, life has become more spontaneous and less rigidly structured, while the concept of success is no longer bound to a fixed, all-encompassing ideal. This is, after all, a world where there are no names yet for some of the jobs our children will do.

It's natural for such rapid progress to be frightening. Even people in their thirties and forties have lived through enough change since their childhoods to feel unsettled by the disjunction between 'then' and 'now'. Innovations like the internet and social media have huge benefits, but they exact an onerous human toll. As Leonard Mlodinow puts it in his book *Elastic*, we have been forced to 'invent new structures for our personal lives that account for the fact that digital technology makes us constantly available to our employers . . . We have to manage ever-dwindling "free" time so that we can interact with friends and family, read, exercise or just relax . . . Everywhere we turn, and every day, we are faced with circumstances and issues that would not have confronted us just a decade or two ago.'[8]

It's a struggle sometimes to believe that the ladder is worth climbing; that Earth might become a better place to live for most of its inhabitants and that any of us might be in a position to help with that. As I said earlier, the ladder symbolises advancement in general. Technical or professional progress must go hand in hand with moral progress. From the Greenham Common protesters of the 1980s to contemporary climate campaigners like Greta Thunberg and female education advocate Malala Yousafzai, women have always been at the forefront of this debate. Like many people I was impressed by the achievements of Gitanjali Rao, who at the age of 15 was named *Time* magazine's Kid of the Year for her work in developing technological solutions to issues like contaminated drinking water and cyberbullying. And I enjoyed talking to the British climate activist Bella Lack for having the fortitude to find optimism in what can feel like a hopeless situation.

The problem is, women have often been at a disadvantage when it comes to buying into visions of the future (or even an idealised present). Think of the 1950s, when the shiny promise of frozen food and automated kitchens did more to shackle than liberate, leaving a hangover of depression and anomie that feminist pioneer Betty Friedan famously called 'the problem that has no name'. Now, despite real advances in areas such as menopause-awareness, too many women remain locked into old routines, fighting the same old battles over pay and childcare and even what brands of feminism are now acceptable.

On top of that we have the pressures of social media and, post-Covid, what even the World Health Organization has felt obliged to call out as a 'blurring of boundaries' between home and the workplace as ideas of hybridity and working from home (WFH) become ingrained across professions. And guess what? It's women who bear the brunt of WFH. As things returned to normalish after Covid (but before Russia's invasion of Ukraine), Bank of England monetary policy committee member Catherine Mann was warning that women who worked mostly from home risked hurting their careers and getting caught in a 'she-cession' as more men than women returned to conventional office working.[9]

Time and again, I've been fascinated by the way my interviewees have reacted to setbacks, often seeing within failure the shoots of future success. The stories they tell me are generally stories of transformation, whether that's turning a rough childhood into accomplished adulthood or overcoming a disability. Women have to learn resilience because they are so often relied upon to demonstrate it in the face of male negligence or incapacity; so often left holding the baby, literally and metaphorically.

When it came to dividing the book thematically into chapters, I allowed myself to be led completely by my *Ladder* guests. Early on we tackle a subject many of them raised – IMPOSTER SYNDROME, the familiar sense of being out of your depth or undeserving of success that so many women experience. From there it's but a hop and a skip to considering different concepts of SUCCESS AND FAILURE and the way we re-evaluate them as we move through life. All ladder-climbing women understand the importance of DODGING THE SNAKES in the form of bullying or predatory men. After that we focus on turning ADVERSITY to your advantage, even when it threatens to overwhelm you – perhaps the most important skill any of us can learn. Finally, we consider the importance of EMBRACING CHANGE: moving beyond your comfort zone and acquiring the ability to adapt.

First things first, though, as we try to answer the most fascinating question of all: How do we become the women we are?

BECOMING AND BELONGING

When do we start to know who we are? At university in the early 1990s, when I was still wearing fluorescent green jeans and drenching my hair with Sun In lightener, I grappled with the notoriously abstruse writings of the French psychoanalyst Jacques Lacan. What he calls the 'mirror stage' begins when a young child first catches sight of her reflection and is crucial in ego formation: that is, shaping emerging perceptions of selfhood. A little later, around the age of three, most of us develop so-called 'theory of mind': the ability to identify others' feelings as distinct from our own.

Lacan pops into my mind, for the first time in decades, when I'm chatting with my *Ladder* guest Carolyn Harris, the menopause awareness campaigner and Deputy Leader of Welsh Labour, born in Swansea in 1960. She tells me her earliest memory was of staring at herself in the mirror in her mother's bedroom and seeing 'a short, chubby girl with long hair and ringlets who wanted to do so much but didn't think she was going to achieve anything'. As she says this, I think: how horribly young to feel such bleak pessimism about your prospects.

'It was very much a male world,' she continues, 'and I had lots of aspirations in my mind that I never wanted to articulate for fear that I would look silly. I didn't want to ask a question in case it was a stupid question. Didn't want to point out my views in case they were the wrong views. That's something a lot of working-class women feel. I wanted to be a doctor, so I went to see the careers teacher. She looked up and said, "Oh dear. Well, that's never going to happen, is it? There are lots of manufacturing jobs available . . ." That was the first time I'd been brave enough to say I had an aspiration and [the rejection] has stayed with me for the rest of my life.'

Ideas about what we might be destined to achieve are seeded early. Tina Stowell, now Baroness Stowell of Beeston, was the daughter of a painter/decorator and a factory-worker, so technically working-class like Carolyn, but the atmosphere she grew up in was very different. 'Where we lived in Beeston Rylands in Nottinghamshire was a close-knit community, a typical working-class area where everyone knew everyone,' she says. However, issues of class difference were never discussed when she was young. 'If anyone came close [to mentioning it] then my mother would always describe us as successful. "We're a successful family." And she really believed that as well. She believed it because of her own upbringing – she was from a very, very poor background. Her definition of success was the security and stability that they provided for us and the fact that we had a dad who was always in work. We might not have been wealthy but we didn't want for anything, and to her that made us successful.'

Becoming is a complex process influenced by both nature (genetics and biology) and nurture (environment and experiences, which include the personal choices about how to live that we make every day). These work in graceful tandem to shape our personalities, beliefs, values and habits. The takeaway from this is not, however, that we drift along being passively shaped by events. It's that we and our brains are plastic, constantly evolving, and have the capacity to change and grow throughout our lives.

In other words, we are becoming all the time. That process includes reviewing who we think we once were, aided by our not-always-reliable autobiographical memories. In the unfinished memoir she began two years before her death, Virginia Woolf described her first memory: sitting on her mother's lap on a train or omnibus, looking at the pattern of red and purple flowers on her black dress. But then another memory surfaces 'which also seems to be my first memory, and in fact it is the most important of all my memories' of lying in bed in the nursery of her family's house in St Ives, listening to the waves crashing on the beach.

The memories are simple and intensely happy. 'I am hardly aware of myself, but only of the sensation. I am only the container of the feeling of ecstasy, of the feeling of rapture. Perhaps this is characteristic of all childhood memories; perhaps it accounts for their strength. Later we add to feelings much that makes them more complex; and therefore less strong; or if not less strong, less isolated, less complete.'[10]

Spice Girl Melanie C makes a great observation when I'm interviewing her at Cheltenham Literary Festival about her autobiography. 'The interesting thing for all of us is that our childhood is our normal and it's not until you get beyond that and start to examine it a bit more closely that you go: Hmmm, actually . . .' Melanie's was different to her friends' because she was the only person in her friendship group whose parents were divorced, something that's hard to imagine now when, as she says, 'it's probably rarer to have your parents together'.

Melanie was born in 1974 in Whiston in Merseyside. Her mother sang in bands herself and Melanie remembers as a child watching her perform and the house being full of rehearsing musicians. The fact that both her father and mother remarried and went on to have other families with their new partners – 'and yet I'm the only child of my mum and dad' – made Melanie feel a little bit uncertain about her place in the world. 'These new families were forming and I felt like a bit of a burden. It was "who's going to have her at this time, who's going to have her at that time". So it made me think: Right, I have to establish who I am in this world. I have to be worthy of this existence and to me the connection you have with people when you're on stage, the love and adoration you get as a performer, felt like the way to go.'

Because we're at our most adaptable as young children, we don't necessarily register bad things that happen to us as bad until later – until someone points it out to us, say.

Ebullient and charismatic, the Right Reverend Rose Hudson-Wilkin, Bishop of Dover, is the first black woman to have become a Church of England bishop. She was born in Montego Bay, Jamaica, and raised there by her father and his sister after her mother left the family home. As she talks to me about her childhood, I'm struck by how accepting she is as an adult of a situation that must have been difficult for her as a child: 'My parents were not married. My father came over from Cuba with his mother and siblings when he was a child and then his mother became ill. So they grew themselves up, which would have been very difficult at that time. My mother is from Westmoreland in western Jamaica. She came to Montego Bay and met my father and they had my older sister and then me.

'At some point, my mother decided that she would come to the UK because she already had three siblings here. I believe the plan was to work and earn enough to send for us. Unfortunately, she found someone else and they got married and started a new life.'

Rose didn't see her mother again until she was nine years old.

'I did speak with her [about why she left] some years ago and she said, "Oh, your father was never interested in getting married" – and who can hold that against another woman? I didn't know it was a traumatic event. I was two years old when she left so I had no memory of her. My father's sister raised us. She assumed the role and she was brilliant. My father was on the sidelines. The trauma of growing himself up [had affected him badly], perhaps because he was a boy. We women usually know how to pull our socks up and get on with life.'

Former Conservative MP Nadine Dorries grew up in the Liverpool suburb of Anfield in housing she says would be condemned today. 'I remember, one winter, breaking ice on the bath to get water because the pipes had burst and my mother had filled the bath with what was left. There wasn't enough money to eat. I can remember sitting up all night with my dog Lassie on my knee, the dog crying because her tummy was rumbling so bad. I remember women in the street cooking in a big pan that had fallen off a big ship and everything going into the pan to feed the kids.'

This experience of childhood poverty set her apart from 'most people I know', she says, especially the likes of David Cameron and George Osborne, who she famously called 'two posh boys who don't know the price of milk'.

'For years I carried around the stigma, the shame of that poverty and how awful it was for me. Now I realise it was fantastic, not least because it's given me all the material I need to become a bestselling author who's sold three million books! It has enriched my understanding of so many issues.'

Our identities are partly constructed out of our relationships with our parents and siblings: shifting tides of attraction and repulsion, inclusion and exclusion. Retail expert Mary Portas grew up believing she was 'the naughty one' in her family, destined always to be beyond the reach of her mother's affection. 'My elder siblings were quite academic and then my third sibling, my brother Joe, was quite arty and also quite quiet.

And I just wasn't. I didn't have this place of affection with my mother. Well, I knew she loved me. But I was pretty full-on. I remember her saying to me once, "My God, if I'd had you first then I think I'd have stopped." Which is a bit of a big thing to say!'

In his book *Redirect*, Timothy D Wilson observes that our interpretation of the world is 'rooted in the narratives we construct about ourselves and the social world, and sometimes . . . we interpret things in unhealthy ways that have negative consequences.'[11]

Those narratives are often passed down to us from our parents. 'Most of us inherit viewpoints from our parents for a period of time,' the novelist Lionel Shriver tells me, 'and it takes us a while to get a sense of perspective and receive information from different places and begin to be your own intellect.'

If these narratives are sometimes restricting, they can also be wise and enabling. Jude Kelly, the theatre director and founder of the Women of the World Festival, was born into a working-class family in Liverpool, one of four daughters. Her mother was a Protestant with German grandparents and her father was from Irish-Catholic stock. Jude's grandfather used to say to her, 'Never forget you're the third in', meaning that the Irish were the 'third in' after the Chinese and West Indian sailors who mostly made up Liverpool's immigrant community at the time.

'I remember going to ballet classes when I was about four in the African centre in Chinatown and having a sense that this was a community of all different kinds of stories and backgrounds. And I loved that. My grandfather meant "be respectful and aware", that [immigration is] a river, a flow. He was a merchant sailor and Liverpool is obviously a port city, with that sense of thrusting forward out to the world and receiving the world back in. There was a greenhouse in Calderstones Park full of rare orchids that sailors had brought back from around the world. I thought Liverpool was the centre of the world.'

Jude's 'mixed' Catholic/Protestant household mirrored the sectarian atmosphere of postwar Liverpool, but without any of the rancour you might expect. '[My parents] were very relaxed and so were their families. We weren't allowed to go to Protestant or Catholic church because it wasn't. fair, so we went to a Presbyterian one instead! So the idea was . . . not of compromising exactly, but belonging to everybody, respecting everybody.'

A woman with a similar story is Rachel de Souza, the former headteacher who in 2021 took up the post of Children's Commissioner for England, promoting and protecting the rights of children. Her father too was Irish Catholic, but her mother was stateless, a refugee from Eastern Europe who was placed in an orphanage near Passau for seven years until *her* mother had remarried and settled in Scunthorpe where Rachel was born in 1968. 'It's interesting with families with these kinds of histories because my step-grandfather was Ukrainian and he'd had his own journey over,' she explains to me. 'He'd been an engineer and was an enemy of the people under Stalin. He came over, got a job in the steelworks, but at night he was a dissident journalist, quite a famous one. We grew up with a lot of languages.'

Studying her family taught Rachel that circumstance makes it harder for some people to 'become' than others. 'For many of the refugees or people who got displaced during the war, their lives almost stopped and they lived in stasis. My grandfather was forever thinking about getting back; my mother was forever wondering who her father was . . . It's not unique. Far more people have these kinds of backgrounds than you realise, especially in many of these industrial towns, I think.'

When individuals form their own identity by separating from their parents, psychologists call it 'individuation'. During this process, people may begin to question the beliefs and values they were raised with and seek out their own. This can lead to a stronger sense of self and a clearer understanding of who they are. But it can also cause conflict and tension within family relationships as they assert their independence.

As a child, I went with my family to church every Sunday and sang in the choir. But the older I grew, the more fed up I got with the absence (at that point) of any female vicars. Questioning it prompted exasperation – 'Why do you need female vicars?' – but also, in me, the first stirrings of feminism.

It's a natural process: children break away and a fault line opens up. Rachel de Souza enraged her Ukrainian step-grandfather by wearing a CND badge to lunch. 'He said, "внучка! If you wear that you're not getting any pocket money!" I thought this was a matter of justice, so for the next six months I wore that badge and got no pocket money.'

In actress Eileen Atkins' case the divide was social and intellectual rather than political. Initially she was close to her father. 'But as soon as I started to be educated at all I became a snob and started to look down on him,' she says. 'I thought: Well, I can't discuss anything with him. There were no books in the house and I had become such an avid reader. He was so angry that I read that he used to sulk when I was reading – I didn't want to hear his stories anymore. I think I was pretty snooty and horrible to him and he was a very good-tempered man.'

Another actress, Geena Davis, was a dutiful child who went to church and Sunday school. Her parents were excessively polite, she remembers, and instilled politeness in their children as the ultimate virtue, to the point where she was conditioned to think she mustn't ever ask for anything. The result was that she 'learned to have no needs at all: even if someone was handing me an already poured glass of ice water, I was to say, "No, thank you. I'm not thirsty."'[12] I wonder, talking to her, if she became an actress in the first place because performance enabled her to be a bigger character than she was allowed to be at home?

'I've come to that conclusion, actually,' she says. 'I told my parents when I was three that I wanted to be an actor. I don't know how I latched onto that. In hindsight, I think maybe it was a way to try on a different personality that wasn't acceptable in real life.' When Geena failed to graduate from her drama degree at Boston University she didn't tell her parents, and kept up the lie that she *had* graduated for years afterwards in interviews, in case they ever saw the article. 'Anything that didn't strictly conform with whatever they approved of had to be hidden at all costs.'

For every woman who defines herself in opposition to her parents or community, either because she wants to or needs to, there is one who acknowledges being cut from the same cloth. Sometimes this admission of similarity is reluctant.

A compulsive traveller, the feminist pioneer Gloria Steinem only realised late in life that her wanderlust was something she had inherited from her father. Looking through his old journals and road maps and address books triggered memories of her itinerant childhood, driving across America with her father as he sold and bartered small antiques to pay for petrol and accommodation at trailer parks. 'Until that moment,' she writes in *My Life on the Road*, 'I would have sworn that I had rebelled against my father's way of life. I created a home that I love and can retreat to, though he wanted no home at all . . . Yet in the way that we rebel, only to find ourselves in the midst of the familiar, I realised there was a reason why the road felt like home. It had been exactly that for the evocative first decade of my life.'[13]

Gloria also realised that her father's ability to live with 'and even love' insecurity, which she also absorbed, had served her well in her career as a free-lance writer.

Children often develop a finely tuned sense of injustice. Born into a working-class family in Chorley, Lancashire, Kirsty Brimelow KC – former chair of the Criminal Bar Association and one of the UK's leading human rights barristers – tells me she first became aware of inequalities within society after witnessing her own mother's exploitation. 'At the time she was managing three jobs and one of those jobs was piece sewing. She didn't work in a factory, she worked from home so that she could see us when we got back from school and she was paid 20p, 50p, for a hem and a zip. I remember one day when I was probably eight or nine years old, it was my job to take her wages off her boss because everyone else was out. I remember he came [to our house] and delivered them in a brown envelope and he said there was going to be a deduction from her money of a couple of pounds, which felt like a huge amount to me. He held up this zip and said, "This isn't straight." And I remember looking at the zip and thinking: There is nothing wrong with that zip, you are ripping off my mum and that is really terrible. It stuck with me because I thought she worked so hard.'

Many politicians I know acquired their sense of political orientation from their parents early on. 'There was a lot of CNDing,' remembers the Labour MP Jess Phillips of her childhood. 'I definitely had CND symbols painted on my face for the entirety of the 1980s. The life I was born into was a political one. My parents made all the posters for the Labour Party in our garage and we made leaflets.'

Jess has said that she gets her loudness and impassioned socialism from her father; whereas her aptitude for detail and ability to juggle family with work are more like her mother, the daughter of a dinner lady who combined raising four kids and several foster children with a senior job in the NHS. Her mother was capable and positive; her favourite phrase was, 'Well, there's probably something we can do.'

Similarly, if you've grown up around parents who ran or founded businesses, you think that's normal so you're more inclined to do it yourself. 'Whatever your parents have done is normalised for the next generation,' says Phoebe Gormley, the first female tailor to open a shop on London's Savile Row. Her father, Rowan Gormley, founded the wine merchant Naked Wines, among other entrepreneurial feats. 'He has always worked so hard and when he isn't working he's reading or always learning. It's so inspiring to see that constant ability to take more on. His father lost his job when my dad was a teenager and that was a really formative moment for him.'

A story I love that Phoebe told me is about the way her parents encouraged her, as a child, to find her identity through play. 'Mum was never judgemental and we had one little room that was the messy room and it never had to be tidied, you could just create chaos in there. Lots of dressing up! I started making my own clothes when I was 14. I had an insatiable teenage-girl appetite for clothes and in the wonderful little town I grew up in there were a couple of pubs, a couple of churches and one fabric shop and no clothes shops. If I wanted clothes, my mum is the most unmaterialistic person ever and her ideal Saturday was surprisingly not driving me to Norwich an hour away to go clothes shopping and I would end up making my own.'

One of the most powerful women in the tech industry, Nicola Mendelsohn, is head of Meta's (formerly Facebook's) Global Business Group, having been VP of Europe, the Middle East and Africa since 2013. Growing up, she remembers a 'loving, warm house but with working women everywhere I looked: Grandma worked with Grandpa running a market stall in Manchester's Arndale Centre selling haberdashery, buttons and bits and pieces. I worked there during the summer holidays. My mum and dad still work together running a kosher catering business, Celia Clyne Banqueting. My mum started off as a home economics teacher, but as she started to build up the business it happened – as it does for so many female entrepreneurs – around the kitchen table. So in the early days my friends and I would be roped into the conveyor belt of making food to scale. She would experiment on us, so we had a lot of delicious meals growing up. Life and work were very much part of the same thing. I never saw the difference.'

Knowing when not to take parental advice or follow their chosen path (or one they have chosen for you) is hugely important in carving out an identity of your own. Minette Batters, the first female president of the National Farmers' Union of England and Wales (NFU), remembers her childhood as a rural idyll: 'Life was very much on the farm. We never had a holiday except for the Royal Agricultural Show, an annual few days away because my father was working there. I remember a black-and-white television that didn't work very well and being rationed anyway on the amount we could watch. A lot of time was spent exploring, building dens. From an early age I had an affinity with cows. I reared calves before and after school.'

It might have seemed as if Minette was on an obvious trajectory towards a career in farming. But from the outset she knew that that was going to be 'incredibly difficult', not least because her father 'didn't like women going into farming'. 'He saw it as a man's world, having grown up at a time when farming was not mechanised. That technology was not coming through so he saw it as an industry about strength, effectively.' He tried hard to put her off, but Minette ignored him, even if friends, too, said it was madness to take over the tenancy of the family farm, as she did in the late 1990s. She wanted the challenge because, as she says, 'the challenges you face in life are how you get success in the end'.

Many of my *Ladder* interviewees have mentioned an important teacher mentor who inspired them to excel. Mine was my English teacher, a man called Harvey Hallsmith who, under the stage name Harvey Hall, had been a popular TV and film actor in the 1960s and '70s, starring in *Z Cars*, *Dixon of Dock Green* and several Hammer horror films before making the switch to teaching. He excelled at wordplay and brought books to life using an array of funny voices.

Born and raised in the district she serves today as MP for Birmingham Yardley, Jess Phillips was a bright child who passed the entrance exam to her local grammar school. 'When I was a kid I really wanted to take the eleven plus,' she remembers, 'because I really liked the competition element of it. When I was four I had a teacher called Mrs Firman whose daughter is still one of my best friends and she made me feel like a clever girl. You know, like "you're a clever girl, young lady", and I really wanted to prove what a clever girl I was all the time.'

'I had a wonderful teacher who taught me Latin,' Helena Kennedy KC tells me. 'He ran the debating society and I remember him saying (I would have been about 12): "A number of you are going to be arguing for the death penalty, and a number of you are going to be arguing against it. Helena, you'll be for the death penalty." And I put my hand up and said, "Oh no, no. I don't want to be arguing for the death penalty. I'm against the death penalty!" He said, "That's not the point of the debate. You have to put yourself in the shoes of someone who is for it." So I suppose he prepared me for the whole business of being involved in legal argument!'

Rachel de Souza 'ticked the box', as she puts it, acquiring enough O-levels to get into sixth-form college, but she 'wasn't a particularly good student'. Not until she was suspended for non-attendance did she realise her academic potential: 'That was a moment where I had to decide: was I serious or not? What was I going to do?'

Instrumental in answering this question was a Philosophy and Religious Studies teacher called Paul Fitzpatrick. 'It was the quality of his teaching, his rigour, but also his commitment to me. No one in my family had been to university.' Out of school she had always been a big reader, particularly enjoying James Joyce and Milan Kundera. One day she went to see Mr Fitzpatrick and told him she wanted to go to university after all. 'He didn't flinch. He just looked at me and said, "Well, there's Oxford; there's Cambridge;

there's Durham. Which one do you want to try for?" I said, "Where did you go?" And he said, "I went to Oxford first, then I went to the University of London, to this college called Heythrop." So I said, "Right, I'll go there" – and I did.'

When Women of the World festival founder Jude Kelly was in her early teens she became, in her words, 'very difficult and wayward'. The person who got her back on track at Quarry Bank High School was Ernest Pobjoy, the headmaster who had performed a similar role for another alumnus, John Lennon, some years earlier, allowing his pre-Beatles band The Quarrymen to play in the school hall.

'He was the only person who stopped me making major mistakes that would have made it very difficult to have the career I've got. In my case he used flattery. I was shoplifting and I was going to go to court and he said to me, "I think you're an existentialist, aren't you?" I had no idea, but I thought: That does sound good. He persuaded me that I needed to read Jean-Paul Sartre and Simone de Beauvoir and that this would make me understand that *of course* I was an existentialist, but that it was probably better to use my talents in other ways. He then said, "What you ought to do is go into the assembly hall every lunchtime and start your own drama group." That became somewhere I could harness my talents rather than my frustrations. It was very savvy of him and shows what good educationalists can do.'

Trying to understand others is the key to understanding yourself. After all, we only exist as social creatures in relation to other people. But this becomes problematic if, for whatever reason, you're different from most of the people around you. Writer Paris Lees remembers always being bullied as a child for being a 'girly boy'. She never felt safe anywhere and always walked around wearing headphones without the sound on, so that she could hear should someone come up to grab her or hit her. This was because 'the way I saw myself', as a girl, 'wasn't the way other people saw me' – as a boy. This perceptual glitch has been an issue for trans people since time immemorial.

Likewise, if you're black but everyone around you is white, the implications for the way you construct your self-image are obvious. Chine McDonald, author and director of the religious thinktank Theos, told me about the time, shortly after she'd moved to south-east London from Nigeria at the age of four, when a teacher asked everyone in her class to draw a self-portrait. 'I remember drawing myself with blonde hair and blue eyes and someone, a friend, looked over and said, "That's not you." I think that was the first moment when I thought: You're right, that isn't me. I don't look like everyone else. And I remember being really disappointed by that, that I didn't look like a Disney princess or whatever.'

The gap between what women look like and how they see themselves is one that affects us throughout our lives and has massive implications for the jobs we do and the relationships we find ourselves in. This might seem a trivial example but as a teenager I saw myself (and was seen by my peers) as nerdy and studious. So it shocked me, when I was working as a waitress in the summer before university, that male customers thought it appropriate to stuff notes in my apron. I stood in the pub toilet, looked at myself in the mirror and tried to see myself as those men saw me – a depressing exercise because they clearly saw no further than my breasts and my blonde hair.

It can take a long time to become who we are. As we progress through life, we slough off false identities along the way, like a snake shedding a skin. This sounds a bit existentialist, but I like the idea that we are always in a state of becoming and can't be defined by a single role. Someone who allows herself to be ruled by an identity imposed on them from outside is said to be living in 'bad faith'. Who wants that?

In *Being and Nothingness*, Sartre explains the concept using the example of a waiter. He asks us to imagine ourselves in a Paris café watching the man serving customers. He is doing his job competently and well, bowing and flirting and taking orders, but there is something 'off'. This is because he is 'playing at being a waiter in a café'. His movements are 'a little too precise, a little too rapid'. He is faking it till he makes it (an idea we shall discuss approvingly in the next chapter as it has its uses) but the difference is, the man is trapped rather than liberated by his performance. He isn't doing the job as he would like to do it, but in the way that he thinks people want him to do it.

'A grocer who dreams is offensive to the buyer,' writes Sartre, 'because such a grocer is not wholly a grocer. Society demands that he limit himself to his function as a grocer, just as the soldier at attention makes himself into a soldier-thing with a direct regard which does not see at all, which is no longer meant to see, since it is the rule and not the interest of the moment which determines the point he must fix his eyes on (the sight "fixed at ten paces"). There are indeed many precautions to imprison a man in what he is, as if we lived in perpetual fear that he might escape from it, that he might break away and suddenly elude his condition.'[14]

For Sartre, only by existing and acting in a certain way do we give meaning to our lives. There is no fixed idea for how a human being should be and, in the absence of a God, the onus for defining who we are through how we act is on us.

This is the terrifying, absurd thing about life. Not for nothing does Sartre talk about 'the anguish of freedom': deciding how to live is a massive responsibility.

In case you think this all sounds a bit blokey, Sartre's lover and fellow philosopher Simone de Beauvoir insisted that women are as capable of choosing their freedom as men. For women the goal is moving beyond 'immanence' – the historical state of women as passive, static and obedient – and reaching 'transcendence', a position where they are able to take responsibility for themselves. She had some skin in the game here. A dutiful Catholic schoolgirl, she was raised in a genteel, bourgeois Parisian family. Her mother imparted her deep religiosity to her children and because Simone loved her she was only too happy to enact the role.

'I was very pious; I made my confession twice a month to Abbe Martin, received Holy Communion three times a week and every morning read a chapter of The Imitation of Christ; between classes, I would slip into the school chapel and, with my head in my hands, I would offer up lengthy prayers . . .'[15]

De Beauvoir broke away from all this when in 1929 she met the rangy Sartre at the École Normale Supérieure. She rejected her parents, railed against the double standards which made it acceptable for men (but not women) to 'sow their oats' before marriage and chose a life of the intellect over one of domesticity: 'I want life, the whole of life. I feel an avid curiosity; I desperately want to burn myself away, more brightly than any other person, and no matter with what kind of flame.'[16]

All of which said, it's obviously easier to move from immanence to transcendence if you're a middle-class white European woman, because the odds aren't stacked against you in the same way. I wouldn't define transcendence solely in terms of academic or professional success, but plainly those things are important. A 2022 report by the Trades Union Congress (TUC) revealed that two in five (41 per cent) black and minority ethnic workers had faced racism at work in the previous five years, often in the form of jokes or banter or comments about their appearance.[17] One of the case studies was a black woman called Mary. 'I work as a lecturer,' she told the TUC's researchers. 'I drive a nice car and one member of staff asked me if I was a drug dealer because how else could I afford to drive the car I drive?'

In 2021, a report by the Fawcett Society found ethnic minority women to be sorely under-represented within senior leadership positions, a result of 'structural racism and barriers faced at each stage in a woman of colour's career pipeline', starting in the education system.[18]

It's all about access, or rather the lack of it. 'I learnt my feminism outside the academy first,' writes Mikki Kendall in her book *Hood Feminism: Notes from the Women White Feminists Forgot*. 'You could almost see the ivory tower from my porch, but while reaching it was supposed to be a goal, there was minimal interaction from the students and staff at the University of Chicago with the residents of my neighbourhood, Hyde Park.'[19]

Sometimes, though, there may be other impediments too. A British Army physiotherapist and medical officer, Preet Chandi, completed a daring solo expedition across Antarctica to the South Pole in January 2022. Even as a child, Preet played tennis to a very high level, moving away from home at 14 first to live with a guardian at Sutton Tennis Academy, then at 16 to move to the Czech tennis player Jeri Novak's school in the Czech Republic where she stayed until she was 19.

'I definitely gained a lot of independence quite young,' she says. 'I remember at 19 feeling like I was very behind everyone else my age because I didn't have A-levels, I didn't have GCSEs. But actually I had a whole load of life experience because I was travelling to all these places in Eastern Europe on my own to go to tournaments. I didn't realise until later in life that I had all this different type of experience.'

As a woman of Indian heritage, however, Preet felt keenly the lack of support from some sections of her own community. For one thing, her parents' divorce when she was ten had been frowned upon. Then Preet made a shock career decision. 'When I came back to the UK [from the Czech Republic] I started an access course.

I remember being told I wasn't smart enough, I was too stupid. Then I remember going into Derby and seeing an ad for the Army . . .' When she joined the reserves, some members of her family were 'not happy with that', but she loved how different and unexpected it all was; how she was being pulled out of her comfort zone all the time.

When Preet progressed to a full-time position as a physio in the Royal Army Medical Corp, the complaining got louder. 'There are so many expectations within my community. People asked, "Why can't you be more normal?" all the time. I think we create our own normal. People may not know what you're capable of. They may also project their own fears onto you.'

On her Antarctic trip she was continually pushed to the limit. 'After the halfway point, I developed a chesty cough that got bad and was feeling very tired. I was in a section where there were a lot of wind-shaped bridges called *sastrugi*. My sled would get stuck and I'd have to get it out. I got so frustrated I screamed, but I couldn't even hear my scream because it was just so windy. I remember sitting in one of the little ditches and I just wanted to stay down, get my satellite phone out, call my partner and just have a little rant because that's what I normally do and it makes me feel better . . . But in those moments I was like, "That's not going to help me because then I'll get colder just sitting there." So I said to myself, "Get up, get the sled out, put one foot in front of the other." In those hard moments it was like a mental prison sometimes. All my darkest thoughts and frustrations would come into my mind, about people who had tried to stop me from doing things or put boundaries in place. I found that difficult . . .'

The story was even worse for Parm Sandhu, a former Chief Superintendent in the Metropolitan Police Service. After thirty years of service, she became the first woman of colour to be promoted through the ranks to that role.

'Up until I was about 15 I had a very normal child-hood,' she says. 'The area I grew up in was very mixed and diverse and so my friends came from different walks of life as well. We had the same goals and outlook on life. I was absolutely Westernised and didn't realise that I was different or that I would be treated differently as I got older.

'The expectations that my family had and that the community around us had of girls was that you would be an obedient wife, a mother and a daughter. And there was no real push into achievement.'

Aged 15, she was forced into an arranged marriage. 'My elder sister's father-in-law persuaded my parents. There was a feeling that if we weren't married off young, we'd become too unruly and Westernised. So by the time I was 16, I was at school doing my GCSEs but married, knowing every evening that I was going home to a man I didn't know who didn't speak English. My first marriage was not happy. There was lots of domestic violence. Again, the expectation was that I would put my husband first but his brothers next. I was at the bottom of the pile. When, later on, I had my son, he didn't feature. It was all about the alpha males in the home. And that wasn't the atmosphere I wanted to bring my son up in.

'If any of them came in late, they expected a freshly cooked meal. You couldn't give them beans on toast or leftovers. You had to cook it from scratch. It didn't matter if it was one in the morning. You were expected to get up and get on with it.

'A concession my father had won at the time of the marriage agreement was that I would be allowed to go to college. So I did go to college, but all my homework, all my coursework, had to be done after I'd tended to the needs of the men in the house first. So there was a hierarchy in the house and I was absolutely at the bottom of that pile.

'During the night time I would try to catch up. I got my A-levels, which was a surprise to me. So I still managed to achieve but it was at the cost of sleep and of any time to myself. I didn't mind that because I enjoyed getting an education, I enjoyed reading, I enjoyed all of my studies.'

It took a long time for Parm to escape from this desperate situation. In the short term, she fled to her parents' house and begged sanctuary. Only grudgingly did they allow her to stay. As she writes in her autobiography *Black and Blue: One Woman's Story of Policing and Prejudice,* her family considered it the 'role of the woman to remain subservient to her husband, and to tolerate beatings if her disobedience made such things necessary'.[20] In the longer term, she managed to get a job at the local DHSS office, then drifted onto the pirate radio scene where she made friends who, when her family threatened her with violence if she didn't return to her husband, helped her escape to London and a new life: 'I took my child in my arms and boarded the bus that would take me away from a life of oppression, and towards the possibility of freedom.'

The forces ranged against Parm – her husband, his brothers, her family – never saw her in three dimensions; never saw her as an independent, autonomous agent with her own thoughts and ambitions. It never occurred to them to empathise with her. Not only did they thwart her 'becoming', or her transcendence, to use de Beauvoir's phrase, but they demonstrated that they themselves had not 'become'. They were like the waiter in Sartre's story, acting out someone else's script.

'Sometimes you have to recognise that the community you've grown up in is too closed, too narrow,' Ann Olivarius tells me. She's the pioneering American-British lawyer who specialises in cases of sexual discrimination, harassment, assault and abuse. Ann endured what she calls a 'really tribal' Italian-Catholic childhood in New Jersey. It wasn't until she left home for Yale University that she realised she needed to respect and 'open her heart' to everyone. Not that she was taught otherwise in New Jersey, but it was 'the absence of that lesson, the absence of meeting people from diverse backgrounds or people who were just different'.

Ann's identity as a feminist and stance on abortion are both rooted in her family life. 'My mother had 13 pregnancies. For the last one, which happened in 1972 when I was 17, she had an abortion, which was a massive thing in my family. She didn't say a word to anyone, to any friends. She only told me because I was the eldest. Of course, my father knew, and his view was that she had murdered, as he put it, his son . . . I remember saying congratulations as that was the only thing we were taught. It was an exciting thing to have another kid in the family, this was a Catholic community and I hadn't been exposed to the idea that a pregnancy wasn't anticipated or necessarily wanted. When my mother told me about the abortion I remember looking at her and thinking: Whoah. You know, I've always heard that that's murder. She asked, "Will you support me?" and it was the first time I had to choose between my mother and my religion. Of course, my mother won out.'

To make matters worse, Ann's father was a domestic abuser who got away with his crimes because he was a product of the broader macho, misogynistic Italian-Irish culture – and because he was a man. 'I think, for me, the day I realised I should be a lawyer and a feminist was one of the times when my mother was pregnant with the last child she actually gave birth to and my father was beating her up . . . The police officer, when he arrived, never looked at my mother, who stood against the wall, clearly pregnant, crying copious tears. Her hair had been pulled out – there was a clump of it on the floor. Her nose had been smashed and there was blood everywhere. Her face had been clawed, she'd been kicked and punched. But the police officer didn't say, "You need to go and see a doctor, you need to go to the hospital". It was as if she didn't exist. Instead, he said, "If I hear from you again, I'm not going to be happy. Stop it." My father's view was that my mother had provoked it, which was always the excuse we heard . . .

'After the police left, my father came at me with his

hand raised, ready to punch me in the face. I stood in front of him and said, "Dad, hit me. Hit me hard. Really take me on and hurt me. Then I'm going to call the police again and I'm going to file charges." I was fourteen. But I said that because I believed in democracy. I believed in law, the idea that the police are supposed to do good things in my naive world. My father looked at me and he said, "Really?" and I could see that he was scared.

'He dropped his hand and for the rest of the time I was in that house until I went to Yale, he never to my knowledge hit my mother again.'

This was the moment Ann realised she had agency and purpose. 'I had no idea I had any power whatsoever. I never thought about life in terms of being powerful. What was power? I grew up in a little bit better than a working-class community. What did I know? I was young and very naive.'

Let's go back to that moment when we stood in front of the mirror as toddlers, having not yet 'become' anything; when we were each our own versions of what the novelist Edith Wharton called 'the little girl who eventually became me, but as yet was neither me nor anybody else in particular, but merely a soft anonymous morsel of humanity'.[21]

Go back and stand before it now and you'll feel very different. Especially as women, our relationship with our reflected image changes over the years. It can make us feel whole and happy. But it can also trigger self-criticism as we scrutinise our appearances for signs of ageing or perceived imperfections.

In 2011, a 28-year-old sociology student at UCLA called Kjerstin Gruys decided to live for a year without looking in a mirror. A recovering anorexic, she did it partly to make a point about the vexed relationship between feminism, beauty and self-image. 'Sometimes,' she wrote in her book about the experiment, *Mirror, Mirror Off the Wall*, 'you have to do something extreme and crazy in order to find balance and sanity in the end.'[22]

I completely understand her motives, but I also think there's something empowering about coming face to face with who you are; about training yourself to look at your reflection and see beyond the lines and spots and wrinkles.

That's where real confidence lies. And the more confident we are in our identities, the better equipped we are to set boundaries and state clearly how we feel about things. We're also better equipped to understand other people, even those we perceive to be hostile or opposed to us. Research suggests that in order to be truly and effectively empathetic, you need first to have a stable, secure sense of self. As the McGill University psychologists Sonia A Krol and Jennifer A Bartz put it, to respond appropriately to another person, individuals 'must recognise that the source of their emotional experience is the other; that is, they must appreciate that the emotional pain they are experiencing is not their own pain but that of the other person'.[23]

Empathy is incredibly important. But it can be tough to sustain and there isn't as much of it around as there should be. This is why, in 2006 in a Commencement speech to Northwestern graduates, Barack Obama talked about an 'empathy deficit': 'There's a lot of talk in this country about the federal deficit. But I think we should talk more about our empathy deficit: the ability to put ourselves in someone else's shoes; to see the world through those who are different from us: the child who's hungry, the laid-off steelworker, the immigrant woman cleaning your dorm room. As you go on in life, cultivating this quality of empathy will become harder, not easier.'

I said at the beginning that to climb the ladder – to improve yourself and your environment – you have to believe that the ladder is worth climbing, that the world might get better and your success might contribute to this. Only by knowing ourselves well can we identify and overcome biases, prejudices and assumptions that might otherwise hinder our ability to understand and relate to others.

While technical progress can and will bring about positive changes in society, it can also lead to negative consequences such as increased inequality, environmental degradation and new ethical dilemmas. (Think of the current angst over Artificial Intelligence.) But we shouldn't just give up. Moral progress can occur independently of technical progress as societies made up of living, breathing human beings work to address historical injustices, develop more equitable social systems and address new moral challenges.

Climbing the ladder is partly about this moral progress: deciding who we care for and how we care for them and harnessing the interconnectivity we see all around us. In his book *Zero Degrees of Empathy*, the autism researcher Simon Baron-Cohen writes that empathy 'means being able to find solutions to what might otherwise be a deadlock between incompatible goals'.[24]

A little empathy is all it takes to stop you seeing other people as alien to you and therefore less deserving, maybe even less human. It's a point the foreign policy specialist Arminka Helić, herself a refugee from Bosnia, makes compellingly about attitudes to immigration.

'Don't think of these people as nameless zombies crossing different countries,' she tells me. 'All of them at some point had a home, their children went to school, they had a street that they lived in, they had friends and relatives, they probably played football just like you do and watched something on TV that they all enjoyed and had a favourite meal . . . They are people just like us and it isn't easy to leave all that and come into a different language, a different culture where you are not necessarily always welcome and where people may look at you as someone who is taking from what belongs to them. Think of them as another human being and think of yourself as someone who is lucky to have been born in this country because it could have been you, it could have been any of us . . . Think about your luck and privilege and honour to live in this country and think about the people who wake up every single day and they live in fear. They have seen and experienced things that you can only imagine. And those people are seeking just peace and stability.'

Not everyone finds empathy easy. For some people,

it's something they have to learn, a muscle you can either exercise or leave to atrophy. I know some people, most of them elderly, who have given up thinking what it might be like not to be them: to be young, for example, or to have hopes and ambitions. Whereas someone like Joan Bakewell, a regular guest on my Times Radio show, is able at nearly 90 to keep across 'now' with stunning acuity; to appreciate that, even if she is coming towards the end of her life, it matters for her successors to inherit the planet in the best shape possible.

Journalism is a funny business because on the one hand, some of its core missions, such as exposing wrongdoing and speaking truth to power, are motivated by identification with the plight of people who are oppressed or disempowered.

But of course, the business of emotional investment is a tricky one where reporting is concerned. I remember being moved to tears when I was interviewing the right-to-die campaigner Tony Nicklinson, who had locked-in syndrome, and for all the importance of calm impartiality in news, it's also okay to feel other people's pain and reflect on it. But don't just take my word for it. As my esteemed former co-anchor Jon Snow has admitted: 'I have cried on the news. I have cried reporting in the field. I'm better for it. One does one's best never to let it show, but if we in public life are not touched by what we witness and experience, then we are not giving a true account of events.'[25]

On the other hand, it's hard to get a good story into print or onto the air without being aggressively focused and goal-orientated. So it's tricky for me that you're also required, as a journalist, to switch off your empathy circuit when necessary. When a plainly exhausted Prime Minister Gordon Brown was about to be turfed out of office but had to do a final round of broadcast interviews, I remember being tough with him and suppressing any pity I felt for him.

It might sound silly, but to switch my empathy back on again I read novels. At least one study has shown that reading literary fiction – and interestingly literary fiction is singled out here, as opposed to other forms of fiction or non-fiction – enhances our ability to understand and share others' emotions.[26] As the writer George Eliot put it: 'Art is the nearest thing to life; it is a mode of amplifying experience and extending our contact with our fellow-men beyond the bounds of our personal lot.'[27]

One of the most dislikeable characters in Eliot's most acclaimed novel *Middlemarch* is Edward Casaubon. He's a pompous, middle-aged scholar, working on a ludicrously grand project he calls 'The Key to All Mythologies'. We resent him because he snuffs the life out of his questing, enthusiastic, more intelligent wife Dorothea. We know his book is ridiculous and will come to nothing – and we know that, deep down, he knows it too. But Eliot helps us to see him in three dimensions so that we understand and can empathise with him.

'For my part I am very sorry for him,' the narrator confesses. 'It is an uneasy lot at best, to be what we call highly taught and yet not to enjoy: to be present at this great spectacle of life and never to be liberated from a small hungry shivering self.'

Casaubon is destined never to 'become' the person he wants to be. That may be a small tragedy, but it is a tragedy, nonetheless.

HOW TO BECOME
AND BELONG

- Set clear, achievable goals: Define what you want to achieve and create a plan to reach those goals. Also, trust your instincts. I was intrigued when the advertising executive Nicola Mendelsohn told me that for a long time she hadn't trusted hers. When she was in a meeting, she admitted, she would often have very long 'conversations' in her head in which she worked out what she was going to say and whether it would sound right. By the time she'd exhausted that process, someone else in the room would have made her point and the actual conversation would have moved on.

- Build self-awareness: Take time to understand your thoughts, feelings and motivations, and work on developing emotional intelligence.

- Experiment with doing an activity that expands your sense of self. This might be simply reading a book you wouldn't normally read. But it might also be seeking therapy to gain new insights into why you think and behave the way you do. It usually takes an outsider to see a pattern.

- Build healthy relationships: Surround yourself with supportive and positive people who will encourage and motivate you. Note too that you get back what you give. TV presenter Kirstie Allsopp puts it really well: 'Always remember that old-fashioned manners really matter. Always know how to spell someone's name. If you arrive early, or stay later, or offer to make coffee, etc., you are not demeaning yourself.'

- Remember: Becoming is a lifelong journey, not a destination. Embrace the process!

2

IMPOSTER SYNDROME

One day, when I was a young reporter at the *Financial Times*, I arranged a meeting with the male CEO of a FTSE 100 company. I hadn't met him before. When I arrived in the lobby of his grand, marble-floored office, I saw him waiting at reception and went over to introduce myself.

'Hello,' I said, thrusting out my hand, as we did in those pre-Covid days. 'I'm Cathy Newman.'

He looked at me blankly. 'I'm sorry,' he said, frowning. 'There must be some mistake. I'm here to meet the *FT*.'

'I know,' I said, feeling myself flush red. 'I *am* the *FT*.'

The man had the good grace to be mortified. In his defence, I think the problem was not that I was a woman but that in my early twenties, as I was when this incident occurred, I looked about 16.

Even so, it's clear to me now that, in any apportioning of blame, most of it should be dumped at his feet. (I couldn't help how I looked. But he could help being patronising and dismissive.)

At the time, though, it was a different story. I thought the misunderstanding was my fault entirely.

It had happened because I didn't look like the *FT*. I wasn't dressed properly. I didn't carry myself properly. I lacked gravitas.

Not long afterwards, I went to meet another new contact for lunch. The fancy restaurant was an alien environment to me and in my panic I thought the waiter, who looked very smart, must be my contact.

'Hello!' I said, bouncily. 'It's good to meet you at last!'

It was hard to know who was more embarrassed when the truth quickly dawned on me that once again I'd not just got the wrong end of the stick but decided the stick was a lampshade.

The thing is, once a hole has opened in your self-esteem, it's hard for it not to widen, and for you to fall into it. Paranoid thoughts swarmed through my brain. I didn't deserve to have my job. I was a total embarrassment. I'd let down my colleagues, my boss and the *FT* in general. All my successes as a reporter had been flukes. Worst of all, people were laughing at me behind my back.

Who the hell is she? The new intern? (I was repeatedly asked to do photocopying by established male journalists unaware I was one of them.) What's going on with her hair?

Quite suddenly, I felt as if I didn't fit. Didn't belong.

And it turns out there's a name for that, although I didn't know it at the time.

Imposter syndrome is a psychological condition in which a person doubts their abilities and accomplishments to the point where she becomes convinced she is a fraud. This conviction holds in the face of all concrete evidence to the contrary.

The syndrome was first described in a 1978 article by two American psychologists, Pauline R Clance and Suzanne A Imes, called 'The Imposter Phenomenon in High Achieving Women: Dynamics and Therapeutic Intervention'.[28] Lots of successful women experience it. Indeed, it often seems to be the most successful ones who experience it the most keenly.

Take Sheryl Sandberg, the former Chief Operating Officer of Meta Platforms and the author of *Lean In*. 'Every time I was called on in class, I was sure that I was about to embarrass myself,' she wrote in that groundbreaking tome. 'Every time I took a test, I was sure that it had gone badly. And every time I didn't embarrass myself – or even excelled – I believed that I had fooled everyone yet again. One day soon, the jig would be up . . .'[29]

Or, if you prefer, the actress Emma Watson. 'It's almost like the better I do, the more my feeling of inadequacy actually increases, because I'm just going, "Any moment, someone's going to find out I'm a total fraud, and that I don't deserve any of what I've achieved",' she told Tavi Gevinson at *Rookie* magazine in 2013. 'I can't possibly live up to what everyone thinks I am and what everyone's expectations of me are. It's weird – sometimes [success] can be incredibly validating, but sometimes it can be incredibly unnerving and throw your balance off a bit, because you're trying to reconcile how you feel about yourself with how the rest of the world perceives you.'

Pauline Clance herself experienced imposter syndrome in graduate school, as she explains on her website: 'I would take an important examination and be very afraid that I had failed. I remembered all I did not know rather than what I did. My friends began to be sick of my worrying, so I kept my doubts more to myself. I thought my fears were due to my educational background. When I began to teach at a prominent liberal arts college with an excellent academic reputation, I heard similar fears from students who had come for counselling. They had excellent standardised test scores, grades and recommendations. One of them said, "I feel like an imposter here with all these really bright people."'[30]

For their paper, Clance and Imes interviewed 150 high-achieving American women, all of them well qualified and highly rated by their colleagues. Despite this, the women attributed their successes to luck and other people's senseless overestimation of their abilities. They often believed that they had, for example, been mistakenly admitted to graduate school because of an error by the admissions committee – that luck or faulty marking had played a bigger role than their abilities.

The bearing our childhoods have on our adult lives is so huge that it's almost frightening to comprehend. Psychoanalyst and leadership expert Manfred FR Kets de Vries thinks imposter syndrome is particularly prevalent in families where parents are overinvested in their child's achievement: 'Individuals who have been raised in this environment seem to believe that their parents will notice them only when they excel. As time goes on, these people often turn into insecure overachievers.'[31]

Although subsequent research has challenged this conclusion, Clance and Imes believed imposter syndrome to be a mostly female phenomenon. It isn't hard to see why this would be the case. As de Vries points out, the gender socialisation that women are often exposed to – for instance, being advised by their parents that they should become nurses or secretaries – 'tends to augment their sense of imposture when their achievements rise above those expectations'.

Something I've noticed is the way women often feel they have to be hyper-competent because if they fail they will have let down not just themselves but all women everywhere. Men, by contrast, never seem to worry about this.

(You'd be amazed by how hard it is to persuade women to appear on *Channel 4 News*. We're always asking female experts on the programme and invariably the majority say, "Oh, that's not really my area", or "I don't think I know enough about the subject." Men rarely, if ever, turn us down on those grounds. The problem becomes self-perpetuating because the fewer female pundits or specialists are seen on TV, the more alien an environment live television appears to other women.)

There's also the small matter of what the psychologist Valerie Young calls 'self-regarding attribution bias': 'A cartoon I once saw said it all. A woman struggling to zip her pants says, "Yikes, I must be getting fat!" A man in the same predicament says, "Hey, there must be something wrong with these pants!"'[32]

In other words, women tend to believe that if they fail at something, it's their fault. Men, not so much. Young quotes Dr Sheila Widnall, a professor of aeronautics and astronautics at MIT and former secretary of the US Air Force: 'Treat a male student badly and he will think you're a jerk. Treat a female student badly and she will think you have finally discovered that she doesn't belong in engineering.'[33]

Whatever the truth of what I admit are fairly broad generalisations, a significant number of the women I've spoken to for *The Ladder* suffered from imposter syndrome at one stage or another.

Ancient rumour has it that a youthful Michael Heseltine sketched out his life plan on the back of an envelope. By 25, he planned to become a millionaire; by 35, an MP; by 45, a minister and by 55, prime minister. He's always denied the story (though its source was his good friend and fellow Conservative MP Julian Critchley) and in the event things didn't turn out that way for him. But people believed it because it sounded so plausible.

By contrast, Baroness Nicky Morgan told me she felt like an imposter when she first became an MP in 2010. 'I didn't know Westminster at all,' she said. 'Perhaps there are some people who arrive and, from the moment they make their maiden speech, feel, "This is where I'm meant to be". I remember making my maiden speech, which was an amazing moment, but at the back of my mind I was thinking: I can't believe I'm actually here. And certainly, the first time I was shown into the chamber to be given a sort of tutorial, which in my case was with Sir George

Young and Harriet Harman, I kept thinking someone was going to say, "Well, you shouldn't be here. Out you go."

'It was an enormous life change. I certainly felt, for the first few weeks: What have I done? I had a two-and-a-half-year-old son, so I was juggling all of that. I thought: How on earth am I going to make this work? It was a massive shock to the system.'

How many men would admit to feeling this way?

'Well, that's the issue. It's much more likely to be the women who admit to feeling it. I'm sure some of the men must feel it too. This is why you build allies, build networks – to get you through those tough moments.'

Nicky was promoted to Economic Secretary to the Treasury in October 2013; to Minister for Women in April 2014; then to Secretary of State for Education a mere two months later. That she accepted the Education job she attributes to the way promotions are awarded in Westminster: a 'very arcane system' which demands an immediate yes-or-no response and therefore doesn't give you the time to doubt yourself.

'If someone had said, "Why don't you apply to be a cabinet minister?" there would have been a myriad of reasons why I'd have talked myself out of it. Again, would men do that? Probably not. But David Cameron didn't give me any time. I sat down in front of him in Number 10 and he said – it was a kind of *X Factor* moment – "I want you to be Education Secretary." And I was like: "Oh! Right! Great! Yes! I'd love to do that." Because I had no time, I said yes. And then you work out how you're going to do it . . .'

Right! Great! Yes! I'd love to do that. Nicky's choice of words is telling. Research by Deborah Tannen, Professor of Linguistics at Georgetown University in Washington, DC found that the way women speak in the workplace often creates an impression of lack of confidence. Her conclusion is that 'ways of speaking learned in childhood affect judgements of competence and confidence, as well as who gets heard, who gets credit, and what gets done.'[34]

Nicky successfully masked her imposter syndrome with a can-do bravado presumably learned in her previous career as a lawyer. But what if you have the sort of personality where that isn't possible? Or you have the additional hurdle of being, say, working-class or trans or a woman of colour?

Clance and Imes' initial sample of 150 women mostly comprised white middle- to upper-class women between the ages of 20 and 45. But the syndrome is by no means a badge of neurotic white privilege. Talking to a group of schoolchildren in London, Michelle Obama told students: 'I still have a little [bit of] imposter syndrome, it never goes away, that you're actually listening to me. It doesn't go away, that feeling that you shouldn't take me that seriously. What do I know? I share that with you because we all have doubts in our abilities, about our power and what that power is.'

Likewise, the novelist Maya Angelou once admitted: 'Each time I write a book, every time I face that yellow pad, the challenge is so great. I have written 11 books, but each time I think: Uh-oh, they're going to find out now. I've run a game on everybody and they're going to find me out.'

Differing from the majority of your peers, in terms of race, gender, sexual orientation or some other characteristic, can fuel the sense of being an imposter. It doesn't help that, in my experience, high-achieving people are often lone wolves who find it hard to collaborate and 'muck in'.

The former Camelot CEO Dianne Thompson noticed the way that 'men will not admit to having mentors . . . They feel: I can do this on my own.'[35] I would say this is equally true of some women, though we can argue the toss about motive. (Is it the case that women don't ask for help because they're afraid to?)

Remembering her early career at IBM, the former Veuve Clicquot Business Woman of the Year Nikki Beckett remarked that what looks like strength often masks an underlying lack of confidence: 'When I was in my early twenties . . . I was always trying to prove how bright I was. It mattered to me much more then that an idea was identified as mine and acknowledged as such. But I have mellowed and have become much more confident in myself.'[36]

This identification of maturity with a growing capacity for collegiate behaviour is all well and good. But everyone deserves the right to prove themselves without feeling they have to overcompensate on account of their gender. In her early career as a tabloid newshound, before she graduated to editing glossy magazines like *Cosmopolitan* and *Elle*, Lorraine Candy remembers how 'you would have to go into news conference with every fact at your disposal and I always thought at the time, as a woman, I had to be not just accurate but double accurate, because there was a sense that I might not know what I was talking about.'

Also, being able to share credit is a luxury many women can't afford, because it often involves their contributions being overlooked or chiselled away. One of the most outrageous instances of this is the story of the celebrated astrophysicist Jocelyn Bell Burnell.

Jocelyn was born in 1943 in Lurgan in County Armagh, Northern Ireland. Her father was an architect and one of the designers of the Armagh Planetarium, which she visited frequently as a child and whose staff encouraged her to turn her gaze upwards into space.

Her enthusiasm for science blossomed early. But for a girl, getting to study the subject was an uphill battle. As Jocelyn tells me, 'Way back in the 1950s, the assumption was that girls were going to get married and be at home, not at work, so what they needed was education in needlework, cookery, things like that. Whereas the boys got to do science.'

This was part of a broader sexism which resulted in her brother being treated very differently. 'At that time in Ireland boys counted for everything and girls didn't count for much at all. So when my mother had a baby boy 18 months after I was born, everybody was hugely delighted and said how good it was that Mrs Bell had had a boy at last.'

I wonder how she managed to blag her way into the science class?

'Well, I didn't, not by myself. I tried, but the domestic science teacher wasn't hearing anything of it. When I told my parents that evening they hit the roof and phoned the head teacher, as did the parents of a couple of other girls. From then on the science class had three girls and all the boys.'

After failing her eleven-plus exam, Jocelyn was sent to a Quaker boarding school in York called The Mount School. Moving to England was 'quite a big adjustment': 'There were all sorts of regulations like you don't walk on the grass – nobody ever explained why – and you couldn't go out after dark – again, nobody ever explained why. So it was quite a big cultural change, but once I'd got over that I got a lot out of that school, yes.'

A degree in Natural Philosophy (Physics) from the University of Glasgow followed, then a PhD at Cambridge where she helped the radio astronomer Antony Hewish and his team build a vast radio telescope called the Interplanetary Scintillation Array.

'It looked like some sort of agricultural frame for growing hops up or something like that,' she remembers. 'It was huge, spread over four acres – the size of 57 tennis courts. I didn't do it alone. Six of us spent two years hammering posts into the ground, stringing the wires up between the posts, the cables and so on. My job was all the cables and connectors. I was spared most of the sledgehammering. But I did enough that I could swing a sledgehammer by the end of the degree.'

And was she the only woman swinging the sledgehammer?

'Oh yes. Probably the only woman in the department.'

Did she mind that?

'I wanted to do a PhD in Radio Astronomy and that's what the set-up was. So you get on with it.'

On 28 November 1967 Jocelyn made a discovery that would change the course not just of astronomy but of her life. Looking through the chart-recorder papers on which were transcribed, in data form, the signals from the radio telescope, she noticed what she called 'a bit of scruff' – evidence of something pulsing regularly out there in the cosmos.

It was a tiny anomaly, but as a scientist she was intrigued. 'You think: What is this? It's behaving like a star, but we'd never seen one behave like that, so what is it? Also, a bit of you is saying, "There must be some rational explanation, a bit of interference or wires crossed somewhere" – because it was such a strong signal.'

Initially christened Little Green Man 1 as a joke, the pulsing astral body turned out to be a neutron star or 'pulsar'. (We have the *Daily Telegraph*'s then science correspondent to thank for the term.) It was what Jocelyn describes as 'the kind of star that had not been known previously to exist – really very small as stars go, about ten miles across, but very dense and heavy. It's spinning and it has a beam of radio waves that as it spins swim around the sky, a bit like how a lighthouse swings a light beam around the horizon. If that beam of radio waves shines on the earth then we see a pulse, then another pulse one rotation later, then another and another. One pulse every spin. Turns out it's also spinning very fast, one spin every second. So this was faster than we had ever expected. We didn't know that stars could do this or that this type of star existed.'

Jocelyn's role in detecting the pulsar was covered extensively in the media at the time, though not in a way that pleased her. Journalists would ask Hewish, her thesis supervisor, about the astrophysical significance of the discovery, then turn to Jocelyn for the 'human interest'. 'What were my waist, hip and bust measurements? Would I describe my hair as brunette or blonde? How tall was I? How many boyfriends did I have? The photographers were asking me if I could undo a few more buttons on my blouse please.'

Having been treated as a bit of secondary fluff by newspapers, you might have thought the scientific community would show Jocelyn a bit more respect. But it was a sexist age and she realises now that by wearing her engagement ring in the lab while she was doing this, she was inadvertently declaring herself unserious, a part-timer. As she says, 'At that time, the ultimate goal was to get married. Once married, you became a stay-at-home housewife kept by your husband. Indeed, if you worked it was shameful because it implied the man didn't earn enough to keep you both. The assumption was, I was going into domesticity as soon as I'd finished in Cambridge. And I didn't twig that this was the way I was being viewed until it was too late.'

Despite co-authoring the original paper announcing the discovery, she was not among the scientists awarded the 1974 Nobel Prize in Physics for their work on pulsars.

With great magnanimity, she dismisses this omission as the unavoidable consequence of a 'demarcation dispute' between student and supervisor – 'the Nobel Prize doesn't normally go to students' – and says she was 'hugely pleased because there is no Nobel Prize for Astronomy and I knew it created a very important precedent and would be good for astronomy in the future'. At the same time, she admits the prize became known among her colleagues as the 'No-Bell Prize' – 'so a lot of people were very indignant on my behalf, particularly young researchers'. The decision may not have been fair, but then it was 'very much of its time': 'Society has changed a lot in the last fifty years. We are almost up to the fiftieth anniversary of that prize.'

The interesting thing is that Jocelyn believes imposter syndrome to have been a hugely important factor in all that she achieved.

'I was convinced Cambridge had made a mistake in admitting me and I wasn't clever enough. My policy was to work as hard as I could so that when they discovered this mistake and threw me out, I wouldn't have a guilty conscience because I knew I'd done my best. So I was being incredibly thorough, both in building the telescope and looking at the data coming from it, which I was doing when all this happened.'

The signal from the pulsar occupied around 10 parts in a million – 'so for every million feet of paper I had to go through, [the signal] was occupying about 10 feet'. To perform this task, which involved scrutinising nearly 30 metres of paper data per night, she channelled her imposter syndrome into an obsessive perfectionism.

'Imposter syndrome can be used to cripple you or to drive you,' she concludes. 'It hit me because I was in part a minority person in physics. So I argue that increasing the diversity of the research community should bring in more people with different backgrounds.

This will strengthen the breadth of view. Research done by McKinsey shows that the most successful businesses have the most diverse senior management. Working with a diverse group, it's more robust and more flexible and more successful.'

In this company, you hope, women do less of the sort of thing I notice every day: batting away praise, being self-deprecating, shrugging off achievements even when they worked hard for them.

The connection between impostor syndrome and perfectionism has long been noticed by psychologists. In this situation, self-esteem is linked to impossibly high standards that you set yourself. High standards are important, of course. Nobody wants to be flown across the Atlantic by a pilot who doesn't think standards matter. But sometimes, in your desperation to belong and receive due acknowledgement, you lose all sense of a middle way. The result is what the authors of a great book my eldest daughter encouraged me to read (after I'd bought it for her!) define as 'problematic perfectionism'.

It's what the outcome would be 'if [a] musician were to ruminate over some trivial mistakes made when playing on stage, forget the positive aspects of their performance, perceive themselves to be a failure as a person and subsequently refuse to do anything for days on end but practise to correct those trivial mistakes'.[37]

The fact that as I write this my dominant thought is BUT TRIVIAL MISTAKES MATTER suggests I've still got work to do!

* * *

In December 1949, a young Canadian sociologist called Erving Goffman rented a hotel room on the Shetland Island of Unst – one of the northernmost of the inhabited British Isles, with a population of around 300. For two months he wandered around Unst observing the local staff interacting with the guests, who were often outsiders from totally different regions and social classes. After a time he moved to a cottage just behind the hotel. He opted to take most of his meals in the hotel kitchen, where he worked part-time as a dishwasher. This gave him an opportunity to observe the staff, who had already decided that Goffman was either a spy or a weird recluse – certainly not the American college student with a special interest in farming that he was purporting to be.

'I tried to play an unexceptional and acceptable role in community life,' Goffman wrote later. But beneath this façade of normality he was incredibly excited, because the Springfield Hotel was, he felt, a place where ideas he had started to formulate about human social behaviour were being enacted before his eyes. He listened intensely to conversations and made careful note of physical gestures and social rituals.

The resulting ethnographic study became his doctoral dissertation, 'Communication Conduct in an Island Community', and formed the basis of his groundbreaking, bestselling book *The Presentation of Self in Everyday Life*, published in 1956.

Goffman's contention is that the self is essentially performative. As we go about our daily business, we continually use dramaturgic practices to give a favourable impression of ourselves.

It might sound like a laboured, self-conscious sort of strategy. But Goffman believed all of us employ it all the time without realising. 'Impression management', as he called it, was the practice of ensuring our identity and behaviour are an appropriate match for the social situation we find ourselves in. Theoretically, we have the power to control that situation – 'the individual effectively projects a definition of the situation when he enters the presence of others' – and yet sometimes, for a variety of reasons, our powers of projection fail us.

This is when imposter syndrome often emerges, when there is a mismatch between someone's identity and what is expected of them socially. Desperate to fit in and exhibit competence, a person might well seek refuge in perfectionism and workaholism in the belief that these will constitute a language everyone understands and so facilitate their acceptance.

According to Goffman, everyday interactions are like staged dramas. In the workplace, especially, we are all engaged in a sustained performance: checking each other out and weighing each other up; making finely calibrated decisions about what information to reveal and what to withhold; and making sure we have the right props to hand.

Individuals are the products of a social system. But says Goffman, who was both a cynic and, interestingly, an inveterate gambler, they are constantly trying to game this system to their advantage, assert dominance or protect themselves from embarrassment.

It sounds a very macho business and, assuming there's some truth in it, explains why imposter syndrome disproportionately affects women and ethnic minorities and – according to Daniel Cueto-Villalobos at The Society Pages, an open-access social science project headquartered at the University of Minnesota – flourishes in spite of, or perhaps even because of, increased diversity and representation. Cueto-Villalobos considers that 'efforts to "diversify" high-status fields like academia, law, and medicine sometimes fail to address the subtle cultural factors that can marginalise and exclude underrepresented groups . . . Scholars emphasise that addressing imposter syndrome should involve solutions that emphasise flourishing and well-being over identity-based inclusion efforts.'

In other words, it's not fair to place the burden for solving this problem on individuals: it's the institutions themselves that need to change.

Educational experts sometimes talk about the 'hidden curriculum'. By this they mean a set of traditional practices embedded within institutions that are least visible to those with the least privilege – and often unacknowledged and unexamined by those to whom they are clear. For example, the Palace of Westminster looked very different to the working-class Angela Rayner, who left school at 16 while pregnant and without any qualifications, than it would have done to upper-middle-class Etonian Jacob Rees-Mogg.

Actually, Angela's take on imposter syndrome is fascinating and characteristically no-nonsense. To understand it properly, you need to understand her impoverished childhood on a council estate in Manchester.

In 2015, Angela became MP for Ashton-under-Lyne, the first woman ever to represent the town in Parliament.

Her memories of her first few culture-clash weeks at the Palace of Westminster are hilariously sharp. 'I'd never seen anything like it,' she tells me. 'I remember I was at an event with a Tory MP and I was talking about horses churning up grass on the estate. And this Tory MP said, "Yes, we've got that problem too, but we've got llamas now." And I went, "What? I'm talking about travellers' horses on a council estate . . ." He was talking about his country estate. I thought: Wow, this is a different world.

'They had all these different words and lingo. In Parliament everyone sends letters congratulating each other on the work they do for their day job, like they're sucking up to each other. I'd get a note saying, "Angela, your speech today was tremendous, you're doing such a wonderful job", and I'd be like, but that's my job, I don't need congratulating . . . It's a weird place to get used to.'

Angela's ascent was swift, rather like Nicky Morgan's on the opposite bench. In January 2016, she was appointed Shadow Minister for Pensions by Jeremy Corbyn, then shortly afterwards to the Shadow Cabinet as Shadow Secretary of State for Education and Shadow Minister for Women and Equalities. Impressive and widely liked, she was tipped as a leader-in-waiting. So it was a surprise to everyone when, in the 2020 Labour Party leadership election, she endorsed her friend and flatmate Rebecca Long-Bailey, who ended up coming second to Sir Keir Starmer, choosing instead to stand successfully for the deputy leadership.

To some observers, this was a classic case of a capable woman not going for the top job because she believed she wasn't good enough. But Angela rejects this interpretation. 'I saw it as what my skill set was. They call it imposter syndrome but I don't see it like that. I like helping others, I don't like being the main dish. I find it hard being in the public eye. Getting praise isn't something I got growing up, I didn't get that nourishment, so it's hard for me to get that much focus . . . I'd gone from being nobody to being somebody and I'd never got used to that. So I didn't want to be the leader. But I knew I had organising skills after twenty years in the trade union movement and I knew that there were things I could do to make the Labour Party shine back in its grassroots again. And if I'm stuck in Parliament I can't do that, whereas if I'm out and about . . . My passion is rallying the troops.'

In her book *The Hidden Curriculum*, Rachel Gable interviewed over a hundred students at elite American universities such as Harvard and Georgetown about the challenges of being, for example, black or working-class or the first person from their family to go to college. Gable discovered that these students were often ignorant about basic aspects of college life; also, that first-generation students sometimes 'passed' as continuing-generation students because it was easier and less embarrassing.

One of those Gable spoke to was a working-class boy from the Midwest called Jake, who rarely discussed his first-generation status but, she writes, 'quickly learned to observe the language and behaviour of those in his new peer group and to either mimic or parry when conversation about pre-college experiences turned in his direction'.[38] On a superficial level his

Goffmanesque impression management was successful. But so intense was the effort of maintaining this new version of himself that Jake began to struggle academically and worry that he might have ADHD.

At the other end of the spectrum is Angela Rayner, whose failure to conform is something she has always been proud about rather than anxious. 'I get so much abuse for my language,' she says. 'I remember once I gave a speech and afterwards a nice little old lady came up to me and said, "Wonderful speech, but it's 'par-tee' with a T." I said, "It's 'par'y' if you're a kid from where I grew up." And if I change and start speaking differently then I'm invalidating [those kids] and saying they're not right when it's fine. You don't have to be perfect. I come out with the wrong words all the time. It's just the way I am and I embrace it.'

Kirsty Brimelow KC still feels that 'at some point someone is going to tap me on the shoulder and say, "Hang on, how did you end up here?"' She found that when she was at the Bar doing her pupillage, she had to learn what she calls 'the ways of communicating' almost from scratch. 'You get that much more if you're within a certain environment, a public-school environment. You come with that confidence and you come with that ability just instinctively to know what to do and how to behave – clear up that cup or make sure that somebody is settled in a certain way. Etiquette, I suppose. That took a while.'

Being a successful actress didn't stop the similarly working-class Eileen Atkins from feeling out of place in some social settings. In her excellent memoir *Will She Do?* – the title tells you everything – she remembers the awkwardness of her wedding to the middle-class, bohemian actor Julian Glover: 'This was two very different classes meeting, and I knew Julian's family, with all their social graces, would manage and mine would be silent with the fear of saying the wrong thing, and secretly resentful that I had put them in this position by marrying above my station . . .'[39]

When we speak for *The Ladder* she tells me it took her until the age of 32 to be accepted, but even then she didn't always feel it. 'When I was a girlfriend of Edward Fox, we went away for the weekend and I was very nervous because it was such a posh house. He said, "What's the matter?" I said, "I'm nervous." And he said, "For God's sake stop thinking you're not good enough."'

Imposter syndrome has a curious, in-between status. It isn't a disorder or a psychiatric diagnosis. You won't find it listed in the current, fifth edition of the *Diagnostic and Statistical Manual of Mental Disorders*. Imposters do feature in some of the most notorious mental disorders, such as Capgras syndrome (where patients believe that a person they know well has been replaced by an identical double) and Fregoli syndrome (where they are convinced that different people in their lives are really a single person who keeps changing his or her appearance). But the truth is, imposter syndrome is commonplace. Occasionally feeling like an outsider is part of being human.

Oxford University biologist Catherine Green, who was part of the team that developed the Oxford-AstraZeneca Covid-19 vaccine, says that for this reason she dislikes the phrase. 'I think we all sometimes feel out of our depth. But if you don't ever feel that then you're probably not pushing yourself hard enough. If you're going to be successful, you sometimes do have to be out of your depth and take on something that you're not entirely sure is going to succeed. I'm not sure I feel like an impostor. Sometimes I feel like I don't know the rules or the situation I'm in or that I could have done a bit more preparation. But if you don't get out of your depth, you're probably not going to make it to the other side of the river.'

(A thought which might be helpful: psychologists distinguish between *syndromes* and *disorders*. Many people who ritualise their lives, particularly in areas to do with time-keeping and tidiness, find the activity beneficial. The rituals they perform might seem extreme to their more happy-go-lucky friends and colleagues, but as long as they don't become a handicap, impeding the person's ability to live normally, we would describe them as having obsessive-compulsive syndrome (OCS), not obsessive-compulsive disorder (OCD). The same applies with impostor syndrome. I would say that most professional women of my acquaintance, especially those with children, have some degree of OCS. It's the only way they can get through the day. But how easy it is, under stress, for one thing to shade into another.)

The novelist Elizabeth Bowen once wrote: 'Anywhere, at any time, with anyone, one may be seized by the suspicion of being alien – ease is therefore to be found in a place which nominally is foreign: this shifts the weight.'[40]

Bowen was talking about herself, but it's a lucid thumbnail sketch of a familiar psychological type: the compulsive traveller. (Think of Bruce Chatwin, who wrote to answer the question he once put to his wife: 'Why do I become restless after a month in a single place, unbearable after two?')

A privileged member of the Anglo-Irish aristocracy, Bowen once said that she felt 'English in Ireland, Irish in England' and at home in neither place. In 1959, after her husband's death had obliged her to sell Bowen's Court – her old family home in County Cork, one of the 'big houses' that signified her class's once-exalted status – she spent three months in Rome researching a book. She stayed at a pensione called the Hotel Inghilterra in a bustling, unassuming quarter between the Pincio and the Corso.

'Banal, affable, ripe to become familiar, this was the ideal Rome to be installed in,' Bowen wrote. 'Everything seemed to brim with associations, if not (so far) any of my own. I began to attach myself by so much as looking. Here I was, centred.' Centred as in neutral – so an outsider, yes, but absorbed into the hubbub of the surrounding scene: 'Radio jazz, a fervent young singer at her exercises, a sewing-machine tearing along, and the frenetic song of a small-caged bird, hooked to a sill, were my sound-neighbours.' Rome was, Bowen declared, 'the ideal environment for the born stranger'.[41]

It would be irrational and overconfident to arrive in a new, unfamiliar place and decide we were a perfect fit. All of us have, at some point, felt anxiety about our relationship to a place (a country, a house, an institution) that we're unable to get a purchase on because we don't know what its rules are or if it values what we have to offer.

But sometimes, particularly in high-pressure environments, we can't or won't stop to admit this. And so we panic.

Perhaps the solution is simply to slow down and find, in our heads, that place where we can go to shift the weight, that 'nominally foreign' place: our own private Hotel Inghilterra.

HOW TO CONQUER
IMPOSTER SYNDROME

- Recognise that your perfectionist, high-achieving nature is partly to blame – and find solace and motivation in that fact.

- Find allies at work and share your experiences with them. You'll feel better for realising that they probably feel like imposters too.

- Focus on your own achievements rather than on how they compare to someone else's.

- Keep track of these achievements and write them down on a piece of paper. Equally, when you get praise from a manager at work, make a note of it. When you're feeling bleak, it's easy to forget that anyone ever thought something you did was worthwhile. But they did.

- Visualise your sense of belonging. Partly this means dreaming yourself into a situation so that you see yourself there. But it also means 'self-talking' – telling yourself in clear, simple terms that you deserve your role. 'Doubt can make you great,' says the designer Anya Hindmarch. 'Accept that it's normal, that everyone has that fear. It doesn't mean you're not going to win through. Embrace the gremlin on your shoulder telling you you're going to mess up because he's there to keep you safe – but get him to turn the volume down a bit.'

3

SUCCESS AND FAILURE

We all want success. But we don't always know what we mean by the word.

Perhaps we mean achieving a specific goal or aspiration, either personal or professional. Or finding fulfilment and satisfaction with our lives and accomplishments and noticing a sense of progress and improvement over time. Or attaining wealth, status, power or some other external marker of success such as recognition and respect from others.

Like most children, I think, I wanted to 'be successful' as an adult and often worried I wouldn't be, even though my definitions of success at that point were rather vague and naive. I appreciated that it would take hard work and the odds would be stacked against me. But the idea that, once attained, success might not be all it's cracked up to be would have struck me as absurd. Recently, however, I came across the literary critic Cyril Connolly's cautionary dictum from his book *Enemies of Promise* and I liked it a lot:

'Success is a kind of moving staircase, from which the artist, once on, has great difficulty in getting off, for whether he goes on writing well or not, he is carried upwards, encouraged by publicity, by fan mail, by the tributes of critics and publishers and by the friendly clubmanship of new companions . . . Popular success is like a palace built for a writer by publishers, journalists, admirers, and professional reputation makers, in which a silent army of termites, rats, dry rot, and death watch beetles are tunnelling away till, at the very moment of completion, it is ready to fall down.'[42]

Although his warning applies more broadly, as we shall see, Connolly is talking about literary success: the sort of success he wanted for himself but never achieved, despite a happy, privileged childhood which he came to believe was part of the problem because he spent his entire adult life being obsessively nostalgic for it.

Part of Connolly's considerable privilege is that he was male. So he was able to entertain the idea of being successful (or not) with a melancholy ease born of entitlement. By contrast, professional success (especially) has always been a fraught arena for women. Years of being sidelined, belittled or refused entry altogether eroded our confidence as much as they spurred us onward.

In 1913, the Law Society refused to allow four women to sit the Law Society examinations. They took the case to the Court of Appeal, but in Bebb v The Law Society it upheld the Law Society's decision on the grounds that women were not 'persons' within the terms of the Solicitors Act of 1843. Not until the Sex Disqualification (Removal) Act 1919 was this over-turned, meaning women were allowed to be admitted to the roll.

Women were welcomed into the workplace during both the First and Second World Wars, to fill the roles left empty by men who'd gone off to fight. But after-wards they were pushed back into the domestic sphere. The 1942 Beveridge Report, foundation stone of the welfare state, declared: 'The attitude of the housewife to gainful employment outside the home should not be the same as that of the single woman. She has other duties . . . In the next thirty years housewives as mothers have vital work to do in ensuring the adequate continuance of the British Race and of British ideals in the world.'

Not until 1970 was equal pay for men and women enshrined in law in the form of the Equal Pay Act, which gave women the right to the same contractual pay and benefits as men in the same employment under certain conditions. But it was toothless and inadequate, covering equal pay for the same work, but not for different work of equal value.

We had to wait until 1975 and the Sex Discrimination Act for it to become unlawful for an individual to be discriminated against in the workplace in relation to selection for a job, training, promotion, etc., because of her gender or marital status.

You can see why a dominant theme of my *Ladder* interviews has been the need to strategise on the profes-sional front, for example by creating a persona that screams 'confidence' so loudly that no one could ever guess you don't have any.

For one thing, the MP Jess Phillips advises, women should stop asking for permission to do things. 'It's always easier to ask for forgiveness rather than permission. As a woman in politics you often feel like you have to ask for permission to do anything – to start a campaign . . . Just crack on with doing it. Don't feel like you have to wait.' This habit of docile waiting is partly why 'all institutions struggle to have women at the top'.

Of course, there are lots of other reasons too.

1) Women usually have more and greater significant family care responsibilities.

2) They are often paid less than men for doing the same or broadly similar jobs and receive less recognition. We could go further and say, as the former Mayor of Ottawa, Charlotte Whitton, famously did: 'Whatever women do, they must do twice as well as men to be thought half as good. Luckily, this is not difficult.'

3) They have fewer mentors. (A 2010 study by *Harvard Business Review* found that women were 54 per cent less likely than men to have a professional sponsor. One hopes the situation has improved since then . . .)

4) Women who make it to the top of their professions have often made huge personal sacrifices (e.g. delaying having children; deciding not to have children even when you want them and can have them) that men in comparable positions have not.

5) In many communities around the world, boys are still taught that they are the providers and girls

the homemakers and those values, once inculcated, shape their behaviour. (A 2019 study by the Fawcett Society suggested stereotyping in childhood has wide-ranging and significant negative consequences for both women and men, with more than half (51 per cent) of people affected saying it constrained their career choices and 44 per cent saying it harmed their personal relationships.)

6) Women still face prejudice in the workplace. (Consider again McKinsey's 2022 Women in the Workplace survey, which found that women were 'leaving their companies in unprecedented numbers' not because they didn't want to work, but because they did. The conclusions it drew are the same as the ones it could have drawn twenty years ago: 'Women leaders are just as ambitious as men, but at many companies, they face headwinds that signal it will be harder to advance. They're more likely to experience belittling microaggressions, such as having their judgement questioned or being mistaken for someone more junior. They're doing more to support employee well-being and foster inclusion, but this critical work is spreading them thin and going mostly unrewarded.'[43])

It's easy to feel depressed and depleted about all this. But what has heartened me over the last couple of years is the number of women I've spoken to who have bucked this trend and, to use an expression I dislike but which is appropriate here, been the change they wanted to see.

After athletics and sport, Karen Blackett's greatest love as a child was television. 'Turning on the TV after I'd done my studies, I was as fascinated by the adverts as I was by the programmes,' she remembers, 'and I'd come up with my own alternative ideas, different jingles. I remember the first ad I saw was the R Whites Lemonade one with the guy in striped pyjamas going down to the kitchen to get lemonade in the middle of the night. I wanted something to do with that world but I had no idea how to get into it.'

That girl is now Karen Blackett OBE, one of the most powerful women – and certainly the most powerful black woman – in the marketing communications industry. She's President of the global advertising agency WPP and holds non-executive directorships at Creative UK, Diageo and the Pipeline, an organisation devoted to helping companies to develop, promote and retain their top female talent. In 2018, she was appointed Race Equality Business Champion as part of the Race at Work Charter in October 2018, helping businesses to address inequality. As if that wasn't enough, she's also Chancellor of the University of Portsmouth, where she studied Geography in the early 1990s.

'I have to be in an environment that allows you to be broad and wide and diverse,' she says. 'That helps my creativity rather than being confined by process and templates.'

Being a single mother with a small baby didn't stop her from becoming CEO of MediaCom – because she didn't let it. Instead, drawing on the Open Blend performance management toolkit developed by Anna Rasmussen, she told the company how she intended to do the job. 'I talked to my boss at the time and said, "I'm as ambitious as I've ever been. I'll be more productive than I've ever been because I've got other things to do once I've finished my work – and I'm going to work in a different way."

'Anna Rasmussen talks about work-life blend rather than balance. It's a blend because work is life and life is work and you have to know how to blend the two or there's a winner and a loser.'

Karen admits she has days when she feels guilty because she hasn't had time to cook her son dinner, but says the main thing is to know when to ask for help. 'There's that saying we all know – that it takes a village to raise a child. [My son] has numerous uncles and aunties who are not blood relatives but who he gets different things from.'

I liked hearing about how Karen's job fulfilled a childhood ambition. I feel as if we often hear that from men, but for women all too often something gets lost along the way. They get the wrong encouragement, or no encouragement at all.

My parents were incredibly supportive of me throughout my childhood but they weren't always sure how to encourage me to spread my wings beyond the world they knew. They, and I, had no idea that journalism was a career for women. Once I'd realised it was, and that I wanted to pursue it, it was an uphill struggle getting a foot on the bottom rung of my own personal ladder. Journalism then, and to a lesser extent now, was a question of who you knew. I didn't know anyone, so I wrote hundreds of begging letters, eventually landing a few days' work experience at the BBC.

I remember being so intimidated by a statuesque blonde presenter (whose name I forget) that I was probably a bit of a liability. We went to film on Hampstead Heath, whereupon the statuesque blonde bounded like a gazelle over a muddy ditch. Attempting to emulate her, I slipped and covered myself in mud. My imposter syndrome blossomed wonderfully after that.

Local newspapers were far less glamorous but much more fulfilling as the lack of staff meant that, despite my lack of experience, I was entrusted to go and dig out stories. The news editor of the *North Devon Journal*, for example, told me to investigate the mysterious discovery of blood on a cliff-top path in the seaside town of Lynton. The police, he said, had launched a murder inquiry. But I started nosing around asking questions and I discovered that what was on the cliff-top path wasn't human blood but goats' blood. A council marksman had gone out at dawn and shot a load of wild goats because the population had got out of control. The problem was, they hadn't consulted anyone and animal-lovers were in uproar. The council had been rumbled.

That scoop got picked up by the *Mirror*. I was on my way!

A stint at *Media Week* followed, where I learned to make contacts, work a patch and, again, land the odd scoop, a knack which took me first to the *Independent* and then the *Financial Times* – now edited by a woman, something that when I was there seemed like a distant fantasy. In that cerebral, journalistically rigorous environment I made lifelong friends, and it provided the platform for the rest of my career.

My editor Lionel Barber encouraged me to try for an award called the Stern Fellowship – like Nicky Morgan, I'd never have put myself forward if it hadn't been suggested to me – which took me to the *Washington Post* for four months. Working for such a respected US media institution was revelatory. Every fact had to be checked and rechecked, every source corroborated several times, and off-the-record quotes were actively discouraged, if not forbidden.

I lucked out too with the news agenda as I happened to be there during the contested 2000 'hanging chads' presidential election. One of my jobs was to travel around the country with the Green candidate Ralph Nader. By the time I returned to London, I'd managed to visit more than 25 US states.

Even from day one of my journalistic life, finding out about that goat cull, I knew it was the job for me. Being a journalist is a sort of vocation, as the Australian-Afghan BBC presenter Yalda Hakim recalled when we spoke for *The Ladder*.

Yalda's childhood story is radically different to mine: I lived in the same house from birth until I left home for university. By contrast, her parents smuggled her and her siblings out of Afghanistan on horseback when she was a baby.

Her father had spent seven years in Czechoslovakia, as it was then, studying architecture. He arrived back in Afghanistan to find a country in disarray. So in the dead of night they crossed the border to Pakistan: Yalda and her mother on one horse, her brother and sister on the other, while her father followed on foot with the people smuggler. The journey took twelve days. After a couple of years they moved to Australia, where her father had a connection. Yalda was raised and started her journalistic career there before moving to the UK and working for the BBC.

Like Karen Blackett, Yalda was gripped by television as a child, but by the news rather than adverts. 'When I watched TV it was documentaries about Afghanistan. I romanticised the whole business of making films. I watched wide-eyed – I was just gripped by it.'

Such was Yalda's passion that in her late teens she did work experience on *Dateline*, the Australian news show featuring the investigative journalist Mark Davis, whose work she had admired so much. Eventually she would end up co-hosting the show with him.

'It took six years! I was so committed, I lived and breathed the job. I spent hours into the night printing out scripts and working out how you put TV together, whether long- or short-form. I shadowed senior journalists and absorbed what was going on. I didn't have the attitude of "I need to be on TV", it was more like "I will stay and lick stamps if I need to, just to be in this environment." Back then we used VHS tapes. Reporters would come back with 12 [tapes of raw footage] and I would take boxes of them home and log their material for hours and days. I had no social life! And then I taught myself how to use the camera . . .'

This was the moment of Yalda's canny, daring, brilliant triumph. Without telling anyone, not even her parents, she set off for Kabul, intending to make the documentary she had dreamed of making. When her parents found out that she was not, as she had told them, only going as far as India and had no network approval for the trip there was 'absolute panic'. They jumped on the next plane to Delhi and accompanied her to Kabul, their first time back since they left, where for the next fortnight her father became her 'fixer' while she filmed whatever she could, including inside an opium den.

The result was the documentary *Yalda's Kabul*, which was showered with acclaim and became the highest-rated programme of the night when it was broadcast by SBS in 2008. 'I was just being enterprising,' she says now, laughing.

Success is subjective. As well as being deeply personal and individualised, it can mean different things at different points in your life. Melanie C nodded emphatically when I asked her if the way we quantify success changes as we age. 'Having suffered with depression, success [to me] is happiness. I'm ambitious and I love my work, but I've been at the most successful point in my career and been so incredibly unhappy . . .'

By any conventional metric, the Spice Girls were extraordinarily successful. They sold over 85 million albums worldwide. They went on several successful tours, including their Spiceworld Tour in 1998, which saw them perform in front of over two million fans in more than 20 countries. They won both Ivor Novello and BRIT Awards and had a massive impact on almost every aspect of British culture in the late 1990s, especially with their popularising of so-called 'girl power'.

Melanie had wanted that success so badly in the beginning.

At 16, she left home in Liverpool to attend a performing arts school in Kent. Her moment of epiphany as a singer came as she was singing 'Chief Cook and Bottle Washer' from the Kander and Ebb musical *The Rink* to her classmates there: 'I felt this is it, this is what I want to pursue.'

Having passed the first audition to join the Spice Girls, she then fell ill for the recall and had to beg her mum to ask the organisers to give her another chance. 'They said, "Sorry, we have the five now." And I thought: Oh well, part of being a performer is learning to deal with disappointment. It happens a lot. So I picked myself up and then a couple of weeks later the call came. "Somebody hasn't worked out, we want to see you again . . ."'

Massive success came almost immediately with their first single 'Wannabe' in 1996 and continued at the same peak of intensity for several years. Despite looking brilliant fun to fans and casual observers, the pop-star life was gruelling to sustain and for a long time Melanie didn't feel she could admit, to herself or anyone else, that she wasn't enjoying it. 'This is the thing. It's so hard in that environment because you don't want to complain. What you're doing is your childhood fantasy. You are living this dream.' Behind the grand façade, Cyril Connolly's termites and beetles were chewing away. In January 2000, Melanie went to her GP and was diagnosed with depression: 'I isolated myself and was so ashamed.'

She had started over-exercising and restricting food, patterns of behaviour she now recognises as stemming from perfectionism. 'I think so many people suffer with this failed perfectionism because we never get there. Thank goodness we never get there, because there's no such thing as perfect, right? But as a performer, as an athlete, that determination to succeed is very important to get you to that place. If it becomes out of balance then that's when the problems can occur.'

Another performer who had huge success at a young age is the violinist Nicola Benedetti, who won BBC Young Musician of the Year in 2004 when she was just 16.

Born in Scotland into an Italian family, she moved to England aged 10 to take up a boarding place at the renowned Yehudi Menuhin School for exceptionally talented young musicians. Like Melanie C, Nicola had known even as a young child that she had a special connection to music, what she calls a 'very visceral, powerful bond', especially to anything slow and romantic – anything that 'had that pathos and heaviness'.

The success Nicola sought is subtly different to the kind Melanie wanted and came with different conditions attached. Part of the problematic perfectionism that crippled Melanie was to do with how she looked and how 'sporty' she was or wasn't. She was judged every day on that, and this was before the advent of social media.

While they have the performance element in common, for Nicola, as for all professional classical musicians, success was less about appearance and more about the hard-won attainment of technique that would make the difference between 'brilliant' and 'really, really brilliant'.

'I remember [going to Yehudi Menuhin] like it was yesterday,' she says. 'I found it very upsetting to be separated from my parents, very scary and disorientating, but the minute the actual lessons started I was interested enough and keen enough to want to improve in playing music to withstand the rest. I always say that to parents: it's all a question of balance. If you have enough love for something you can withstand all sorts of things, but if the love you have for it isn't strong enough then those things become unbearable [and] really wear you down . . . It's very relative to how you feel towards either the overcoming of adversity or what it is you're focused on. What is your goal and your priority?'

Nicola rejects the idea that she was a child prodigy. 'It's not modesty. I was talented and very keen and interested and dedicated – I could practise for hours a day at a very young age – and I had an excellent violin teacher. In fact, I had excellent teachers throughout my life who really supported and inspired that love for playing. The Young Musician final was a daze, actually. I'd felt quite stressed out in rehearsals because the piece I was playing, Karol Szymanowski's Violin Concerto, had a huge orchestra, trombones and trumpets, huge percussion . . . It was incredibly dense, therefore it's hard that young to really understand how to prepare for the amount of noise an orchestra is going to make when you're just one little violin; how you're going to be heard above all that noise. It wasn't until it got to the actual performance, before which I did not sleep at all, that I was able to just be calm through the concert.'

But the real vulnerabilities didn't start to emerge until after she'd won Young Musician of the Year. 'The pressure came more like a year later when I started doing a lot of concerts. I was booked to do a lot of performances and proceeded to do some of them well and some of them really badly and was getting a load of either lukewarm or bad reviews.

'It wasn't just the bad reviews I minded – though they did hurt me, because I was so young and wasn't used to that level of public criticism – but also the reviews that would try to predict your future: journalism that takes how you perform in one concert and [on the basis of that] says that you will never be X, Y or Z, or you should never have done X, Y or Z. The reaction in me was [to double down] in determination . . . I mean, I knew I wasn't playing great. I had a fluctuating standard onstage and a lot was left up to chance.

'When I say that, I was preparing meticulously, far too meticulously actually. I would practise for hours and think I could prepare in a way that meant I could control every little thing I did onstage. Actually, though, I wasn't addressing the larger picture of psychological preparation, emotional preparation, general confidence-building and belief that I was meant to be where I was.'

How did she do that?

'It took a long time. I didn't actually start improving until I stopped studying with anybody and took myself out of that subservient student position. Because I was always a very good student, I would absorb like a sponge what I was being told. I was incredibly influenceable, so I would change the way I held my bow or the way I made a sound in an instant. But that's also dangerous because you're not really building a base of how you feel with your instrument and what your own voice is.'

In classical music, success can only truly be attained through hard work. There aren't any meaningful short-cuts. So you have to shape that intensity into a virtue. 'Find your area of most intense curiosity and try to go deeper in that direction,' advises Nicola. 'Have discipline. Try to force yourself to do things that you don't want to do. However, when it comes to something like music there has to be a level of love and appreciation there. The best combination of things you can come up with is where a challenge and a bit of an uphill battle is matched with that deep love you have. Out of that comes the deepest fulfilment.'

I love this and agree completely: I too think success is sweeter when it hasn't come easily. I remember how surprised I was when the former First Minister of Scotland, Nicola Sturgeon, told me how she felt her whole career was a conscious attempt to go against the grain of her natural personality. A shy, studious child, Nicola spent the duration of her fifth birthday party hiding under a table reading a book ('which is what I would still choose to do, given the opportunity').

'That shy five-year-old, believe it or not, is still a shy almost-fifty-year-old, even though she's sitting here talking to you as First Minister [as she still was when we spoke in 2021]. I was bossy with my sister and probably my parents, but to the rest of the world I was pretty shy and still am.

'I've always had that combination of being shy and quiet and an inner resolve. I always knew what I wanted to do and achieve. The most difficult aspect to me has been overcoming that natural reserve – going into a roomful of people I don't know and talking to them. I handle that better when I'm making a speech to people than when I'm conversing normally, maybe because there's a performance element to that. I've struggled to overcome that over the years. Maybe you overcompensate a bit so that the determination has to be greater to overcome that reserve. I don't know. I'm not a psychologist!'

Still, I suggested, you pushed yourself so far out of your comfort zone that you ended up as First Minister.

'Yeah!' she laughs. 'Maybe someone should have warned me! I suppose there is a bit of that. I think you overcompensate for the bit of your personality which, if it was left to rule the roost, would hold you back. So from a young age I tried to do that. I remember at university working really hard to overcome a sense of not being sure if I was up to it and having to force myself to carry on.'

We're back to impostor syndrome. But to put the counterargument, is this a healthy way to think about success? That in order to achieve it you have to edit yourself and put on an act? Sure, it's important to shapeshift, force yourself out of your comfort zone, etc. But it's just as important to keep redefining and reframing the very concept of success.

'Success for me is not about getting to the top of

the ladder,' Tina Stowell says, emphatically. She had a circuitous journey to her post as Leader of the House of Lords, starting her career in the Civil Service, then progressing to the Downing Street press office, then trying and failing to get into Parliament. 'Success to me is about always doing a good job, whatever that job is, and understanding why that job matters and making a difference because you will get so much satisfaction from doing that and other people will notice.'

Top judge Lady Brenda Hale says a similar thing. 'My main advice is to enjoy whatever it is you're doing now because if you enjoy it that means you'll work hard at it and do your best at it. Be the best you can at what you're doing now; then, when other opportunities come your way, even if they haven't been planned, be flexible, go for them, take them on, even if you do feel troubled about whether you can. Because if it doesn't work out, you can go and do something else. There is always something else to be done.'

'Try not to imagine having a career, just have a life,' agrees Jude Kelly. 'Find out what you want your life to be about. Then find a way of making that life happen in the thing you love doing. People get terribly trapped into "my career ladder should look like this".

'Even the word "top" in "top of the ladder" is complicated. I do want women to be as ambitious as they want to be and not to feel as if it's a bit dirty to want power, money, legitimacy, agency, because it comes down to what values you will employ when you have this power. So don't avoid the idea of power because you think it's too toxic or difficult . . . But I also think you can't know what other aspects of life are going to bleed into you. You need to be porous to life. You're going to have tragedies and sadnesses; things that will confuse you, changes of mind and changes of heart, and if your mind is always "my career, my career" then there's a chance you'll blunt your ability to empathise with yourself.'

Of course, loss and failure on your way up the ladder doesn't mean you *won't* end up with a glittering career. Jude has. So too Rachel de Souza. But before Rachel became Children's Commissioner she was a headteacher in a variety of failing schools. Her benchmark for success was not how far she personally advanced but the degree to which she could turn those schools around and help the students fulfil their potential by raising their expectations of what they could achieve: 'The talent and ability in all our children is amazing. You just have to not see the barriers. Go through them.'

Successful people have often gone through the fire of failure first. Often that failure, for want of a better word, has occurred in childhood. Writer and presenter Clare Balding was suspended from Downe House boarding school for shoplifting. She had felt she didn't fit in there as her family were not wealthy: the fees were paid not by her parents but by the American philanthropist Paul Mellon, whose Derby-winning horse, Mill Reef, her father had trained.

This counted for nothing with her posh, rich classmates, who laughed at her unfashionable clothes and joked that she smelled. 'I so wanted to belong to their gang,' she writes movingly in her brilliant, bestselling memoir, *My Animals and Other Family*, 'but they largely ignored me and it seemed impossible that I could ever win their friendship unless I impressed them by being even cooler, even more daring, than they were.'[44]

'I talk to a lot of children and I do understand that feeling of "Everyone hates me, everyone is talking about me, I will never recover from this",' she says. What's revealing is 'how you do recover and reinvent yourself and find the strength of character to pick the better path . . . You can't make people like you. Everyone knows that feeling of trying too hard. And it's not a case of not needing to try, but of turning your vision outwards. The world is not only about you. I've found that if I stop looking at my navel or having the mental camera on selfie mode, and instead look outwards, it is so beneficial. Look out at the world and go: Wow, isn't the world amazing, aren't those people interesting. The minute you make it about other people and not about yourself it can change in a much better way.'

Learning to take advantage of the right breaks at the right time is key to driving success, as Davina McCall tells me. She had had a tricky time of being a young adult, drifting into heroin use until her friends intervened to help her quit. Always a livewire, she was at her most persistent when trying to get a job in TV before she got clean, but realises now that, had she had the success she craved at that point, she would have messed it up through not doing the job well.

She had been bugging MTV for three years to give her a break. 'When the guy from MTV said, "Please stop calling me," I said, "I'll stop calling you if you give me someone else's number". They said, "Okay, here's

XXX's number, can you start annoying him?" So I called him and two years later he called back [with an audition offer] and said, "Okay, this is your moment." I was six months clean and I was thinking – and this is AA speak – it was my higher power rewarding me, saying, "You've done a good thing, well done . . ."'

Writer Sue Cheung was born in Nottingham to parents who had emigrated from Hong Kong to open a Chinese takeaway. Her childhood was defined from a young age by the obligation to work – she describes herself as a former 'child slave' – in her parents' shop. ('As soon as we were old enough to hold a knife without chopping our fingers off, we were out to work in the kitchen,' she told me.) As well as racism from the customers it became her job to serve, there was the constant threat of violence from her taciturn father.

Escape came when Sue was 16, in the form of a magazine competition she won. 'The prize was a scholarship to the London College of Fashion. My entry was a line drawing of a face. You had to put some make-up on and what I'd done wasn't conventional. I'd done a futuristic, arty-farty mosaic. When I was called up as the winner it was amazing because it meant I could get away from the toxic environment that was my family and forge my own future away from the family business. I was hoping it would be the launching pad for my career . . .'

So it was, in a way. But Sue's life in her twenties and thirties followed a chaotic path. While she experienced moments of personal and professional success, the legacy of her abusive childhood prevented them from coalescing into something consistent and satisfying.

First, her bedsit burned down, which resulted in her becoming homeless and falling in with a crowd of squatters in King's Cross. She became pregnant, which led to her being disowned by her family, then encouraged to move back in with them, then cast out again . . . Despite developing a drink and drugs habit, she managed to get a job as Art Director at an advertising agency in Central London. There followed several years of hard partying before she and her husband quit London and settled in Dorset where a new phase of her life began: writing and illustrating children's books.

'It was a love of mine all my life and I really wanted to make a thing of it. I had this pile of ideas that I'd been saving up over the years but I'd never done anything with them.' Partly, this was to do with an incident at school that had shattered Sue's confidence. 'When I was 13 or 14, one of our English teachers pulled me to one side and asked me if English was my first language. She'd read a short story I'd written – creative writing was my favourite subject apart from art – and she said my writing was terrible! [As a result] I binned my writing and concentrated on my art until I was in my forties.'

It took Sue three years to find a literary agent who would take her on. But once she had, a deal followed soon afterwards and after producing several picture books for children she decided, with encouragement from her agent, to write a memoir of her childhood. *Chinglish* was published in 2019.

Part of the book's success for Sue is the way it has given her a chance to talk to children in schools and, as she put it to me, 'opened up this whole conversation about the generations of British-Chinese/South-East Asians who have come over, opened up catering businesses and have similar stories to tell'.

Another thing to bear in mind about success is that it can be maddeningly random. Before she struck commercial gold with the bestselling *We Need to Talk About Kevin*, Lionel Shriver had written six well-reviewed novels that didn't sell in huge quantities. 'I'm often asked, "How did your writing suddenly take this big leap?",' she laughs, 'but all the other books are written by the same person and in many ways equally good. Possibly there was something about the concept of this book [Kevin], it had a standard commercial hook and that probably helped . . .

'When you publish books and they don't sell you're assembling the equivalent of a criminal record. I was discouraged [by her previous books' failure], anyone would be, but then I'd get another idea . . . It would take off in my head and I wanted to write it. That's what pulled me through – that, and spite.'

Joan Bakewell began her career at the BBC as a studio manager, a job she admits she 'wasn't very good' at. 'At the end of the [traineeship] course you took an exam, which I failed. The BBC in those days was generous enough to let me take it a second time. That kind of generosity hasn't survived in today's media . . . Because I was a studio manager I was required to understand a lot of technology and I still don't understand technology, so it was making me unhappy.

'So off I went and tried to be a supply teacher. Then I fetched up in advertising, but I was rather high-minded and disapproved of it . . . I messed around looking for what I wanted to do, looking inside myself, and I remembered I'd seen people arrive at the BBC carrying scripts, reading them into a microphone and going away with a cheque for £10, so that's what I did.'

Joan quickly became a successful presenter, anchoring the pioneering discussion BBC programme *Late Night Line-Up*, which launched in 1964.

Success might come in a different form to how you imagined. This often means acknowledging your limitations. Screenwriter Abi Morgan grew up in an acting family yet 'quickly realised I couldn't [act] for so many reasons . . . I was really bad. I could never do that light-bulb thing that actors do, they just transform. And I could never transform and I love watching actors transform with the work I write and make it utterly their own to the point where I forget I've written it. I realised that was a much more interesting place to be – behind the camera, behind the stage, in the rehearsal room.'

What she did take from her actress mother, however, was attitude. 'She was very "take it on the chin, go into the room, you can do this". She made it seem like an adventure and invariably you can put a rosy glow on that experience . . . She was an incredibly hard worker and when she wasn't acting she was caring, she was working in shops, she was cooking, doing drama lessons after school for kids. She did everything she could do to keep the wolf from the door because my parents' marriage broke up when I was about 11 or 12. She was raising three kids largely on her own, so I watched someone with a really strong work ethic. So yeah, she's been really inspirational, a backbone, and as life's gone through twists and turns she's still working in her eighties, still acting.'

Few women have the luxury many men have of being able to focus single-mindedly on their careers. Often women are forced to juggle work and personal commitments; forced to give up a budding career and take on the lion's share of childcare because their male partners are earning more. (The gender pay gap is still a thing, no matter what Jordan Peterson's followers might tell you.)

I'm lucky enough to have a husband who works from home and has always been able to cook, shop and take the lead on childcare. Even so, there are times when I stretch myself to snapping point.

In her memoir *A Woman's Work*, Harriet Harman describes the white-knuckle ride of fighting her first General Election when her first baby was only four months old. Her second pregnancy coincided with her moving to the front bench for the first time. The next General Election was called in 1987, when her third child was four months old. Not only was she anxious to guard against the perception that motherhood limited her ability to be an effective MP, but she had no systemic support whatsoever.

'Now, it is expected that MPs and ministers will take a period of leave when they have a baby . . . But in the eighties, with me the only MP having babies, there was no maternity leave from the front bench, let alone from the pressing needs of my constituents.'[45]

Despite her successes, she 'fantasised about giving up': 'My maternal guilt was exacerbated by the contrast between my life and that of what I imagined to be the wonderful "earth mother" who was able to flex her work around her deeply contented children, or who didn't work at all.'[46]

Like Harriet, I've always compensated for my work absences by straining every sinew to do all the things full-time mums do for their children, even if that ends up leaving me feeling frazzled.

The implications go deeper than mere tiredness, however. A recent survey by the British Chamber of Commerce of more than 4,000 women found that as many as 67 per cent of them felt that childcare duties in the past decade had affected their career progression, including missing out on pay rises and promotions. At the same time, the Trades Union Congress has calculated that nearly 1.5 million women are kept out of the labour market because of their responsibilities as carers, compared with just 230,000 men.

I was struck when I was researching my book *Bloody Brilliant Women*, a history of 'forgotten' British female achievers, by something the feminist historian Deirdre Beddoe wrote in her book about women's lives during the interwar years, *Back to Home and Duty*: that women's goals and political activities in the gap between the First and Second World Wars were until fairly recently neglected by historians: 'It is as though "the woman question" was solved in 1918, when women over thirty were "given" the vote. Thereafter we are left to assume that women's lot improved and proceeded quietly and inexorably along the road of progress.'[47]

In fact, progress was slow and fitful. The Representation of the People Act excluded a large number of women, and it wasn't until the Equal Franchise Act of 1928 that they were granted voting rights on the same terms as men. Although women entered the workforce in large numbers during the First World War to replace men serving in the military, afterwards many of them were pressured to leave their jobs to make way for returning soldiers. Not only were marriage and motherhood considered the primary roles for women, but contraception and family planning were highly restricted during this period – as we would expect in a society that was still stiflingly patriarchal.

An optimistic reading of the last twenty years is that things are moving in the right direction. It's now easier for women to be successful across a range of different spheres. More women than ever before have access to education at all levels. More organisations and governments than ever before recognise the importance of diversity and gender equality. (Say what you like about the UK Government's FCDO International Women and Girls Strategy 2023 to 2030, but at least it exists.) More women are serving as CEOs, board members and political leaders.

More generally, women's achievements in science, technology, sports and the arts are being acknowledged in a way they simply wouldn't have been even at the turn of the millennium. One woman who has given her all to ensuring this is so is the redoubtable Jude Kelly, whose thoughts on what inspired her to celebrate female success and aspiration I found fascinating.

'My grandmother left school at 12 and had 14 children, so within three generations a Liverpool girl is Artistic Director of the South Bank Centre, one of the great classical arts venues. That's a phenomenal journey of social progress. But when I got there [in 2006] and looked around, we had the Hayward Gallery, the Purcell Rooms – most of the work was men's artistic history and creation. It was still, broadly speaking, feeding an idea of the canon that is male, white, European and doesn't reflect the story of others.

'It was a time when people were saying, "Oh, we don't need feminism, we've done that." We were just coming out of lad culture, which was dismaying, and I was seeing all these women who weren't being given opportunities artistically or in lots of other ways . . . Then it was the hundredth anniversary of International Women's Day in the UK and I decided to do this one-off festival, Women of the World, celebrating not just the arts but women in every walk of life: journalism, health, law, cleaning ladies, unions, whatever; to take this idea that there are a thousand stories that need to be told and if we heard each other's stories then we'd understand the world we need to create together.'

I wondered if she still feels that women's rights are under strain?

'When people have a central idea that your rights are conditional on their permission, then first of all they're not too bothered when you do a bit of moving [forward] towards more rights. Then they tell you how far and no further you will go – and when you trespass across *those* barriers then there is pushback. You can see that very strongly at the moment in various ways.

'When you expose something that's got pus inside, so to speak, people get very angry and an element that wasn't there before is social media. When women say "we are going to have equal power", the ugliness of the assault is horrific. It's the same with Black Lives Matter – you're okay as long as you're doing something that the ruling group feel is okay. Step outside your lane and all bets are off.'

She's right. Whenever I cover a story or conduct an interview that touches on women's rights, the ferocity of the reaction on social media is extraordinary. I've been called a cunt and a bitch, turned into a meme on Pornhub. My favourite tweet from a troll was this: 'When I look at you I see the devil looking back.' The response from one supporter was priceless: 'Should have gone to Specsavers.'

Of course, the world changes for women in a way that it doesn't for men as they hit menopause, usually in their forties and fifties. For our mothers' generation this was the Great Undiscussable, a source of deep shame and embarrassment. It was the point at which women, having lost their fertility, were supposed to put their ambitions behind them, step down a gear professionally and fade gracefully into middle-aged invisibility.

Back in the early 1990s, when editor Joanna Goldsworthy was seeking contributions to a book of personal essays on the menopause, she encountered a good deal of resistance. 'Refusals from potential contributors I've approached ranged from, "Oh, I had no trouble at all. It affected me so little I don't have anything to say about it," through, "I really don't have time/I haven't *had* it yet [outraged to be asked]," to, "I don't want to admit to it."

'*Admit to it*? Well, there's a thing.'[48]

That so many now *will* admit to it and more is thanks to the sterling work being done by a number of high-profile women like Davina McCall and my Times Radio colleague Mariella Frostrup. When we spoke Davina had just published her award-winning book *Menopausing*, co-written with Naomi Potter, and presented a groundbreaking Channel 4 documentary on the subject. I loved her insistence that it's not enough for women to wait until they're perimenopausal themselves to think about what's coming down the track.

'If you're under the age of 40, there is something you can do. Just as you can have a post-mortem, I believe in having a pre-mortem and there are certain things you can pre-empt and account for before they happen. When you're in your thirties, go to your local GP and say, "Who is the specialist healthcare professional who deals with women's health at this surgery?" And if there isn't one, spend the next ten years getting one because you'll be doing every woman in your area the most amazing service. There are around 60 symptoms because oestrogen affects every organ in your body: your brain, heart skin, ovaries, joints and bones. You might have palpitations, or maybe dry eyes and a dry mouth and it's very hard to join the dots at our age: all these separate little things could be one thing. You want to make a note of anxiety and depression you experience because one in four women are prescribed antidepressants for menopause symptoms and that's a statistic that needs to change.'

Research by the Chartered Institute of Personnel and Development (CIPD) found that nearly 60 per cent of working women between 45 and 55 with menopause symptoms felt it had a negative impact on them professionally.[49] They were less able to concentrate, experienced more stress and felt less patient with clients and colleagues. Nearly a third of women surveyed said they had taken sick leave because of their symptoms, but only a quarter of them had felt able to tell their manager the real reason for their absence, either because they were embarrassed or because they believed their manager wouldn't understand.

I've been pleasantly surprised by how many of my *Ladder* interviewees felt that they were at their most successful as older women.

'There's bags of confidence that I didn't possess twelve years ago,' says the Conservative MP Caroline Nokes. 'There is almost a determination to be deliberately contrary, to be challenging and outspoken. And I think for women, sometimes that's really difficult, particularly for women in their fifties. We're doing a whole load of work on the Women and Equalities Committee at the moment around the menopause. Women are talking to us about loss of confidence and anxiety and so I almost feel it's incumbent upon me to make sure that that doesn't happen to me. I can continue to be out there as a woman who is going to say exactly what she thinks, without fear or favour.'

Eileen Atkins says that unlike some of her peers

ageing 'hasn't been tough' for her as an actress. 'I've either been lucky or maybe searched a bit more and been readier earlier to say, "I'm not a young girl anymore." Striving to be young if you're in my profession is absurd. Everybody knows how old you are! People might stand around you and say goodness, you look amazing because the work that's done has been good, but you still won't get the young parts because the young ones will come along and quite rightly take the young parts.'

Another Great Dame, Maureen Lipman, is still doing great work in her late seventies, and lots of it. When we speak she has just taken a month off from playing battleaxe Evelyn Plummer in *Coronation Street* to star in Martin Sherman's one-woman show *Rose* in the West End. Her performance as the Holocaust survivor who finds a new life in America won her some of the best reviews of her career. Maureen calls it 'the most miraculous piece I've ever done. It's everything an actor or a patient audience could want.

'It's going to kill me,' she jokes. 'I wish I wasn't getting older. I don't like the holes in my face, but I'm too scared to do Botox. Which actresses do I admire for ageing well? Diane Keaton. She's got old in a kooky way. Andie MacDowell. Ali MacGraw. Ageing isn't to do with grey hair, it's to do with acceptance.'

'It's a marathon, not a sprint,' agrees the veteran Labour MP Margaret Hodge. 'Some of my most successful years have been my later years. So the idea that you've got to get it all done before you're thirty – just hang on, you've got a long, long time.'

HOW TO BE SUCCESSFUL
(FINGERS CROSSED)

- Remember that success isn't a single, monolithic thing; that it's subjective and changes with age.

- Stop asking for permission to do things. Men don't ask for permission. (Okay, some of them do. But way fewer than women.)

- Visualise success. I find a good way to do this is to remember something you felt passionately about as a child and try to recover that sensation. If you can remain in touch with that primal emotion, you're halfway there.

- Know your worth, including your actual monetary value. Several senior businesswomen have mentioned to me that, in their experience, young women especially do insufficient preparation around their annual reviews. I certainly didn't, back in the day.

- Don't fear a particular outcome, especially ageing, which can be so much more satisfying and enjoyable than you think.

- Ask for help. Kate Bingham, Covid vaccine procurer: 'There's always a hesitancy to do this because people think it makes them look weak. But if you don't ask, you won't know what the answer is.'

- Value your own happiness. Sue Cheung: 'If you don't put your own happiness first, what good are you going to be for anything? If you are happy then everything around you is going to work out better. Always put yourself first. I know it sounds selfish, but it's not.'

- Be prepared to be disappointed sometimes. Creative work, especially, can be a slog before you hit a successful streak. Actually, it can be a slog *even then* . . . Lionel Shriver: 'Only [write] if you really enjoy the process, and I don't mean the process of sending it out, I mean the process of writing the book. If that is not in itself an active pleasure, do something else.'

4

DODGING THE SNAKES

For women, there are snakes everywhere. Always have been, always will. I suppose it's a question of visibility. It would be nice to think there were fewer of them than there once were. After all, the last decade has in many ways been a turning point for women. Across the world, we have risen up to challenge traditions and orthodoxies that kept us marginalised, the #MeToo movement being the most obvious example. And we have had, if not scores, then at least a decent handful of female leaders in the worlds of economics and politics, from Christine Lagarde (President of the European Central Bank) and Ursula von der Leyen (President of the European Commission) to Jacinda Ardern (former Prime Minister of New Zealand), Joyce Banda (former President of Malawi) and, um, Liz Truss (former Prime Minister of the UK).

But merely becoming a leader doesn't protect you as a woman. Because it's often then, when you've reached the highest point, that the snakes slither out of their rocky homes, as the former Prime Minister of Australia Julia Gillard noted in *Women and Leadership*, the book she co-authored with Ngozi Okonjo-Iweala, Director-General of the World Trade Organization. When she became Prime Minister, Julia 'assumed that the maximum reaction to my gender would be experienced early in my period of office and then it would all normalise to business as usual'. In fact, what she found was 'the longer I served as prime minister, the more shrill the sexism became'.[50]

The font of this sexism was, more often than not, opposition leader Tony Abbott, who ran against her on a 'ditch the witch' ticket and notoriously responded to a question about the desirability of women having power with this: 'Yeah, I completely agree, but what if men are, by physiology or temperament, more adapted to exercise authority or to issue command?'

This culminated in the woman who was doing a perfectly good job of exercising authority and issuing command delivering what became known as her 'Misogyny Speech', denouncing Abbott in the strongest possible terms: 'If he [Abbott] wants to know what misogyny looks like in modern Australia, he doesn't need a motion in the House of Representatives, he needs a mirror. That's what he needs.'

Climbing the ladder means removing your blinkers and being attentive to the point of hypervigilance: not just to overt misogyny but to systemic biases and prejudices; also to predatory or even violent behaviour that may be so subtle or unexpected that we don't initially recognise it as such.

'Many people have preconceived notions about the

nature of sexual assaults,' write Kristi Gray and Dorislee Gilbert in an essay on sexual assault prosecutions included in the survey of misogyny *Hating Girls*. 'If you asked an average citizen to imagine what a rapist looks like, they would likely come up with a masked intruder or a man who drives a van with no windows. A stranger to the victim. Someone who "looks creepy" and has an untreated, severe mental illness or, at a minimum, severely compromised social skills. A man who is either unemployed, works varied menial jobs, or is some kind of weird tech-savant. It's unlikely that [they] would envision a Stanford University swimmer, a beloved television star or a hospital internist.'[51]

These assumptions are dangerous in themselves, but also because of the way they influence the outcome of sexual assault cases in the criminal justice system when they are held by jurors, police officers, lawyers and judges. I've always regarded this so-called everyday sexism – a phrase that has entered the lexicon thanks to the sterling work of Laura Bates, founder of the Everyday Sexism Project – as the thin end of the wedge. Failure to crack down on it forcefully is what allows institutional sexism to flourish.

Laura is clear when I speak to her that you have to tackle the whole spectrum, from harassment to sexual assault. 'I really wish that all the people who say that, you know, wolf whistles are a compliment and catcalling isn't a big deal would talk to some of the 10- and 11-year-old girls I've talked to who are in tears because they feel so unsafe – because an adult man old enough to be their dad or their grandfather is, in one real example, shouting from their cars for the "girl with the dick-sucking lips to come here" as they walk to school. If anybody thinks that's meaningless and harmless, then I'd really like to understand why.

'What we're doing is setting up a power dynamic. If we say catcalls and wolf whistles are meaningless – that girls should enjoy them, blah, blah – what we're essentially saying is that girls' bodies are public property, and there's nothing they can do about that. If you look at the stories on the Everyday Sexism Project website, you see the same language thrown at women, the same words come up again and again, whether it's the story of a woman being abused by her husband behind closed doors or illegally discriminated against in the workplace. No one is saying these things are all the same. No one is saying that one leads directly to the other or that they have to be punished in the same way. But yeah, of course, they're connected. Of course they are.'

Laura had left Cambridge University, where she studied English Literature, and was working as an actress when she endured, in short succession, a series of sexual assaults. It was these that catalysed her career pivot into activism and advocacy.

'I was on my way home when a man started following me,' she remembers, 'and started quite aggressively sexually propositioning me, refusing to take no for an answer and saying, "I know where you live, I'm going to follow you and there's nothing you can do". Within a few days of that incident, I was on the bus quite late at night on my way home, on the phone to my mum, when a man completely unexpectedly put his hand on my thigh and then between my legs. I panicked and froze for a moment, but because I was on the phone I blurted it out: "I'm on the bus. This guy just groped me." And everybody on the bus heard and everybody looked out of the window. No one said a word. No one stepped in, no one confronted him. But it was almost more than that. They didn't even look at me. It felt like they were saying, "Don't bring this up. This is your thing to deal with." Then, a few days later, I was walking past some guys on the street and one turned to the other and said, "Look at the tits on that." It was that sense of dehumanisation and invisibility, but more than anything the normalisation; because what I realised at the end of that week was if those three things hadn't happened in the same week, I wouldn't have been sitting there thinking about them because it was so normal.

'I thought back to university, where there was a supervisor who wore a black armband every year to mourn the day when women were admitted to the college. And I thought back to being lined up and rated out of 10. I thought back to so many experiences and it was kind of like a train hitting me: Why is this normal?'

As a Generation X woman whose working life began in 1990s Fleet Street, I suppose I grew inured to workplace sexism. My leaving university coincided with the peak of lad culture: *Loaded* magazine, Britpop, the rise of the 'ladette'. 'Post-feminist' women were expected to play along, laugh at the banter and go for drinks where you matched the blokes pint for pint. Female cultural role models included Bridget Jones and Ally McBeal – thirtysomething professional singletons defined by their fraught office-based relationships.

I can think of several men – senior colleagues on

papers where I worked; men twenty or even thirty years older than I was then – who behaved towards me in ways that strike me now as shockingly inappropriate.

I remember attending one of the political party conferences, bumping into a national newspaper editor at the bar and, on leaving to go to bed, getting a phone call to my room asking if he could come and share it as his chauffeur had inexplicably done a runner . . .

Meanwhile, the atmosphere in the lobby at the House of Commons, where I was based as a political reporter, was in those days like a boys' public school. I laugh when the Conservative MP Caroline Nokes uses exactly the same phrase to describe it when we speak for *The Ladder*.

'I hadn't really experienced sexism until I came [to Westminster]. I'd been the younger daughter of a man who only had daughters and I went to an all-girls school. I worked in an organisation before I came here that by accident rather than design only employed women. And so this place was a real slap in the face. What I experienced was direct sexism. It was people saying, "Well, you've only been made a minister because you've got tits." Just deeply, deeply offensive and really patronising. These "little girl" attitudes, a lot of condescending behaviour and pretty blatant examples of direct sexual harassment and bullying; them using their influence and alleged "seniority" as tools with which they would put you down.'

Looking back, I'm astonished by the things I put up with. When a peer I occasionally met for lunch – he was a useful contact; sometimes, in journalism, you just have to hold your nose – texted me in advance to ask me to wear the long boots he liked, I would simply sigh and roll my eyes. (No, I did not wear the boots.) Quite often, as a woman, you found yourself in weird situations where you were made to feel you'd used your 'charms' in an underhand way, especially if you came away with something the men didn't. Perhaps this is why one former Labour cabinet minister once described me to his colleagues as 'the Mata Hari of political journalism'.

Because yes, sometimes being female made you stand out in a way that gave you an advantage. A bizarre example: I remember attending Labour's party conference in Blackpool in 2002. At a dinner where guest of honour Bill Clinton was present, someone on my table dared me to ask him for his autograph. As I walked towards him, the grey sea of male suits parted to grant me passage. The former President caught my eye and winked at me before willingly signing my proffered box of official Labour Party peppermints. (He didn't actually say 'suck it and see', but he might as well have done.)

And of course there's the constant low-level stuff, the stuff every woman has to endure, like the buzzing of a fly in a room. The man at the private members' club who came up to me when I was sat waiting for someone at the bar, put his hand on mine and said, 'That's sexual assault, then, is it?' The emails from 'Mike', of which this is an example: 'Last night's *Channel 4 News* was a treat, you decked out in your silky nylons. You may be hated by Twitter/X but I adore you and your silky nylon legs. I could wank over that all night.'

Thanks, Mike! Glad to be of service!

It's hard to know whether this stuff is better or worse than what Joan Bakewell experienced in the 1960s and '70s. 'That was a time when women were assumed to be available in a sense that is unacceptable now,' she admits. 'It was considered acceptable [then] to hug a woman, to squeeze her around the waist and stroke her bottom. This was considered not overfamiliar but a social behaviour that was acceptable, pushing the edges.' (Ironically, the comedy writer Frank Muir, who coined the term 'thinking man's crumpet' to describe Joan, was, she insists, a decent sort – 'not one of those men at all: he was seemly, tall, thin and witty.')

In those days 'you simply used social mechanisms to avoid [harassment]', such as not getting in the same lift as a man you knew was a 'groper'. Joan has courted controversy by suggesting contemporary attitudes are too rigid and draconian. 'I've seen us arrive at a situation where when someone puts their hand on your knee their career is ruined. I sometimes feel that there's no leeway for an occasional intimacy. Touch is almost illegal and I find that almost harsh. Perhaps that's because I'm older and no one is touching me anymore!'

I know what Joan means, but sadly the grey areas she's talking about are catnip to a certain type of predatory man. When the 2022 Gender Equality in the Workplace report by the recruitment company Randstad surveyed 6,000 working adults, an alarming 32 per cent of women thought their careers had been affected by sexual harassment. But an even more alarming 72 per cent of women had either encountered or witnessed inappropriate behaviour from male colleagues at work.

The most problematic sectors were construction and tech, with almost half (45 per cent) of women in construction and 42 per cent of women in tech saying that sexual harassment had either a lot or some impact on their careers. Another male-dominated industry, energy, has issues too, as I know from my *Ladder* conversation with the engineer Nina Skorupska, chief executive of the REA, the association for renewable energy and clean technology.

I loved hearing about Nina's childhood in Radcliffe, Lancashire as the daughter of working-class Polish immigrants.

'Radcliffe was once described as the ugliest town in Lancashire. It seriously was. It had loads of paper mills, flowing all the different colours of inks into the River Irwell. But my home life was happy. My parents both worked in factories, my father in a paper mill where he worked shifts – 6 a.m. till 2 p.m., 2 p.m. till 10 p.m., 10 p.m. till 6 a.m. – in a three-week rota. I had the wonderful pleasure, when I came home from school, of my father opening the door and he would have a mug of coffee for me, which was a bit of a no-no for an eight- or nine-year-old, some jam on lovely white warm bread from the local shop and then a list of 20 maths questions. He had had no education because of the war but he was one of the brightest men I knew. So he made this a special game for me, because I was like an only child. Both my older sisters had left home because they were 14 and 12 years older than me. My eldest sister was the first in the family to go to university – she studied Chemistry and Maths at Salford – and then my second sister was a nurse, so there was no lazing about for the women in the Skorupska household.

'I remember being inspired by some of the things my mum said when we were standing around the kitchen sink, wiping the dishes. She must have had a tough day in the factory with some bossy guy and she said, "If you want something, don't expect any man to give it to you, go out and get it for yourself." I loved science and maths at that stage and I became a big *Star Trek* fan, so of course I turned the famous phrase round from "to boldly go where no man has gone before" to "where no woman".'

Nina studied Astronomy and Astrophysics at Newcastle University before realising she preferred Chemistry and switching to that. After a stint in the US studying coal geology she returned to Britain to do a PhD, then went into the energy sector, rising to become nuclear power company RWE Npower's first ever female manager of a UK power station, in this case Didcot B. The lack of female toilets – 'you had to walk miles' – turned out to be symbolic of general attitudes towards women and working on power stations.

'Some of these guys had never worked with a woman and you might think, "What's the problem?", but this was alien, absolutely alien, to them. So it was a novelty, but I didn't want it to be novel, I wanted it to feel normal. So I talked football with them in the morning: I am a big supporter of Aston Villa . . . But yes, if they overstepped I had to overcome the wobbles in my stomach and discipline these 60-year-old guys who'd been working in the industry in maintenance and as operators for a very long time.

'I had to convince people that I was serious. There would be snide remarks from the other station managers. People said, "Oh, you were always the favoured person to be presenting at corporate events, all you had to do was shake your pretty blonde head, Nina, and everybody would jump." I found that hurtful to the point where, and I'm sorry to say this, I went home that weekend and dyed my blonde hair brown. I really did not want anybody to perceive that I was progressing through the organisation because I was a woman.

'There were snide remarks about whom I'd slept with to get to where I was . . . It was all said jokingly, but behind every joke is a query and a question and a challenge. You had to deal with it and say, "Well, obviously it wasn't you", you know. That was the way I tackled that one. By the way, I'm blonde again now.'

I could have filled this book with stories of workplace sexism and I have to say I've been tempted. Of those told to me by my *Ladder* interviewees, perhaps the most brazen involved the senior member of the Bar who gave a young Kirsty Brimelow a less-than-appropriate welcome present for joining his chambers: a négligée. 'It's unbelievable now,' she says. 'He found me in the library and gave it to me. I was then taking advice from everybody about what to do with it. I actually got conflicting advice, but obviously I gave it back.'

The most bizarre tale came courtesy of the conductor Alice Farnham, who has done exceptional work encouraging women to enter this traditionally male sphere. She was informed, in all seriousness, by an eminent male conductor that 'the problem with female conductors is they can't conduct very well because their breasts get in the way'. When Alice laughed at this, the man doubled down and, she says, 'started talking about the high levels of testosterone you needed to show power on the podium'. It was a stark reminder to her that, even if he was in a minority, there were still a lot of men who thought like him. And because of them, women still 'need to be better than the men' to make the progress they deserve.

The Australian feminist theorist Kate Manne addresses this sad truth in her book *Down Girl: The Logic of Misogyny* but finds that even the female urge to excel can be problematic. 'Such excellence in a woman may have the opposite effect on some people,' she writes, 'resulting in her being a polarising figure. In other words, women may be penalised for being too qualified, too competent.'[52]

Manne finds the worst misogyny is reserved for female political leaders such as Hillary Clinton and Julia Gillard, who aspire to masculine-coded social roles. And even when societies become less sexist – 'that is, less sceptical about women's intellectual acumen or leadership abilities' and less inclined to accept gender stereotyping – the misogyny can go underground, resurfacing at specific trigger points and often in a more bilious, concentrated form.

But while misogyny can be brutal and overt, its sneakiness (snakiness!) lies in the way it can also be bat-squeak subtle; the odd comment here and there. The issue is what lies beneath those comments: a system of power which, if allowed to grow unchecked, wraps itself around institutions like Japanese knotweed.

That misogyny has been around since the dawn of time doesn't make it any more natural. As Sandy Doyle observes in *Trainwreck*, her witty examination of the way society treats so-called 'hot mess' women who have undergone very public unravellings: 'Where we now have conservative blogs ranting about Hillary

Clinton's lesbian affairs and/or murder sprees, we used to have poems run in conservative newspapers about how Mary Wollstonecraft – yes, her, the *Vindication of the Rights of Women* lady – was a suicidal hooker with a shame-baby.'[53]

As we've seen elsewhere in this book, there has been a lot written recently about menopausal and perimenopausal women being badly served by doctors. One of the reasons is that modern medicine often feels as stubbornly patriarchal as it was in ancient times, when the ancient Greek physician Galen wrote: 'Just as the human species is the most perfect of all the animals, within the human the man is more perfect than the woman.'

Think of how many women's ailments have, over the years, been dismissed as 'nerves' or 'hysteria'. It's bad enough suffering from depression or premenstrual syndrome (PMS) these days, but imagine having to endure it in the 1930s when even magazines that were supposed to be on your side were recommending fresh air and exercise as a cure. I love this from a 1932 edition of *Woman's Own*:

'Few housewives realise what powers they possess and how much depends on them . . . If she [i.e. the housewife] takes this nervy condition in hand in its early stages, she will prevent disaster in the future not only from the point of view of her own health, but because she is risking something none of us likes to lose – the power to keep her husband.'[54]

Attitudes cement bias. And bias runs through institutions, as Caroline Criado-Perez demonstrated so wonderfully in her bestselling book *Invisible Women*. She argues that healthcare systematically discriminates against women, leaving them 'chronically misunderstood, mistreated and misdiagnosed'.[55] For example, she found that women were 50 per cent more likely to be misdiagnosed after a heart attack but only made up 25 per cent of participants across 31 landmark trials for congestive heart failure between 1987 and 2012.

Like many women, I've experienced this healthcare sexism myself. I was 13 weeks pregnant and had learned from a scan that the baby had an extremely rare condition which meant it was highly likely to die before birth, or during labour. If it survived, my husband and I were informed it would most probably be paralysed, deaf, blind and unable to speak. So after a lot of thought we made the painful decision to terminate the pregnancy.

But as I was waiting for the anaesthetic to take effect outside the operating theatre, the consultant compounded my sense of loss and guilt by offering me advice on contraception, as if I were a teenage mum and this was an unwanted pregnancy – despite my medical notes making very clear my circumstances. His cold, patronising tone was upsetting and I will always be grateful to the kindly nurse who, after I explained to her what had happened, insisted he apologise the minute I came round after the operation.

Dame Helen Stokes-Lampard is, among much else, Chair of the Academy of Medical Royal Colleges. She was Chair of the Royal College of General Practitioners between 2016 and 2019 and has a range of health-related interests, particularly concerning women.

Remembering the misogyny she encountered after she left medical school still makes Helen angry. 'The worst sexism was when I chose my house jobs. I'd got to the end of training at medical school and I was trying to choose my next step. Just to be clear, I didn't intend the route I took. I intended to do a surgical speciality . . . and I remember asking one of the surgeons I worked with if he would consider taking me on as his House Officer. He asked me to come to the operating theatre and he gave me a very humiliating public interview in front of other people. He even asked for a full frontal photo of me when I sent in my CV. I held my head up and laughed it off at the time and swore to myself that I would never work for such a person and that I would call out anything like that if I ever heard it again, irrespective of the power differential . . .

'This was thirty odd years ago. But I remember catching the theatre sister's eyes and seeing a look of pity but also of solidarity. I knew I wasn't the first and certainly wouldn't be the last, but that sort of behaviour now would bring you in front of the General Medical Council very quickly, I think. Junior colleagues are far more empowered to speak up.'

Helen thinks it's vital to 'sort out harassment where you see it happening to other people' and cringes to remember an occasion when she omitted to do this.

'Several years ago now I was in a significant position of professional leadership and was hosting a meeting where, right at the end, an older male colleague made an outrageous comment which was disrespectful to women,' she explains. 'The implication of it was that you would only succeed if you were an ethnically diverse woman who wasn't heterosexual. And there in the room with us was an ethnically diverse woman, very successful, who actually happened to be heterosexual; but I was so shocked, I couldn't quite believe what I'd heard. It was right at the moment when people were starting to leave the room so it was a bit chaotic and then I caught her eye and saw the look of horror on her face. And I was paralysed as I realised I had heard correctly. However, I didn't say something immediately. So she stood up and said something and walked out. And I was then having to pick up the pieces. She was so hurt that I hadn't acted immediately and spoken out. But in the subsequent days we worked it through and the individual who'd made the comment gave the most fulsome apology I've ever heard. It was a powerful learning experience for me to never stand back when something is so obviously wrong.

'There are ways to deal with difficult situations. Some involve an overt "that is not right, take that back immediately or explain yourself". But there are also more subtle situations, and these are perhaps more common, where it's a [matter of saying a] quiet, "Do you realise how that came across?" or "Do you think that's sending the right message about our values?". I've had that conversation many times and I'm glad I have, but it takes courage to do these things and sometimes courage is a thing you have to learn, as well as the resilience to do difficult things.

'You need to build up your armour plates. I think of myself as an armadillo, or more accurately, a pangolin! I've got a soft underbelly, but I've had to develop those plates and scales like armour, to deal with difficult stuff over the years.'

We've all had to do that more over the last ten years, as the ferocity of online abuse directed at women has increased. So many of my *Ladder* women have talked about this and I've experienced my fair share of it too.

Twitter/X has been a cesspool for as long as I can remember, which is why I use it much less nowadays. After my interview with the right-wing psychologist Jordan Peterson several years ago I received multiple death threats, I was 'doxxed' (my home address published online) and my teenage daughter stumbled across a porn meme someone had mocked up of me on Instagram (as problematic a platform as Twitter/X in key respects). Indeed, whenever I post online, I know that even now, when America wakes up, scores of Peterson's young disciples will respond with gleeful trolling comments. It's their right, of course, but it does make many of these social media platforms hostile environments for women.

Women are often ambivalent about seeking success that raises their profiles because of online abuse they know they will suffer. It isn't hard to understand why so many women are reluctant to go into public-facing roles in politics when you read that a single woman, Diane Abbott, received 45 per cent of all abusive tweets sent to female MPs in the six weeks before election day in 2017, or that the veteran Labour MP Dame Margaret Hodge received 'tens of thousands' of abusive tweets a month, most of them viciously antisemitic, while she was trying to push through the Online Safety Bill, which will require social media giants like Facebook to quickly remove illegal content like revenge porn or hate speech or face hefty penalties and even criminal prosecutions.

'The only way I've ever been able to deal with attacks is to compartmentalise my life,' Margaret says. 'I know it's not the real me they're attacking. It's not the me of my family, my children, my interests in theatre, cooking, all the things I pursue at home. It's a me that's been painted by others. And I think if you can do that and understand that it's not the real you that's being attacked, that's the way you can cope with it.'

The worst of it is the way that women dealing with digital abuse find it almost impossible to hold their attackers accountable. When they try, they are obliged to waste hours of their lives wading through comments and messages, trying to document the abuse so that they have proof it actually happened. At the root of this blindness is what, way back in 2011, the sociologist Nathan Jurgenson christened 'digital dualism': the idea that our online lives and our 'real' physical lives are distinct, separate spheres. Women know only too well that this has not been the case for a very long time.

'Women who have succeeded too well at becoming visible have always been penalised vigilantly and force-fully and turned into spectacles,' writes Sandy Doyle.[56] Her point is that it is easy for women to lose control of who they are, and for the way they are discussed and written about to become grotesque. This is part of the ritualised 'shaming': they become known for their sexual partners or their mental health problems or their drug use. This can be true of men too, but as she says, 'Men have to work harder to get to this point. And they have more options when it comes to redeeming themselves.'

One of Britain's best-known and most eminent lawyers, Helena Kennedy KC, has practised at the Bar for over forty years in the field of criminal law. *Eve Was Framed*, her stinging critique of the criminal justice system as experienced by women, is as relevant now as it was when it was first published in 1993.

She speaks eloquently about the sense of entitlement felt by so many men. 'It's that [sense that] there is male primacy, that somehow women are there in a secondary role and often to service and pleasure men. When we talk about misogyny – and I can say this as a classicist! – it's about more than hating women. It's also about having lower expectations of women, denigrating women and not valuing women as equals. That's the basis of all this stuff. It's about the fact that, you know, a young woman can be at a bus stop and a man comes up and says, "Oh, you're looking very nice tonight" and she ignores him. And then he gets angry and starts being abusive. And then he starts getting more abusive and it feels threatening and frightening to the woman who's standing there and she starts having to look and see if other people are around . . . And that's the life experience of women.'

Helena knows more about this aspect of women's lives than most people. That knowledge fuels her anger that female victims of sexual violence are so often let down by the courts because, as she has written, 'when the legal system fails, or is seen to fail, in the fulfilment of its practical function, society reaps the consequences'.[57] Laws and the way they are enforced have enormous power to shape behaviour. So if a judge describes a rape as 'a bit anaemic as rapes go' or declares that a victim was 'asking for it',[58] it isn't just repulsive – it actively blunts comprehension of what has occurred: 'At public meetings, the police and officials often talk about "people" who experience domestic violence, using language which disguises the reality that in our society it is women who are most often battered, women who are killed by their partners at a rate of two a week . . .'[59]

'We all know that thing of being suddenly afraid and also of having to organise our lives in ways that might prevent those things happening to us,' she tells me. 'But it shouldn't be necessary, and men have to step up and actually be our confederates in countering this, calling it out when other men are doing it and bringing up our sons to not think that the world belongs to them and not to women. In a patriarchal society power was in the hands of men, the writers of laws were men, and now of course that's changing but not at the speed that young women expect. So we do have to do something about it and the endgame of degrading women is that women end up being the people who are killed.'

Helena believes we shouldn't waste our time grading different forms of misogynistic abuse in terms of severity because 'it's all swimming in the same water'. 'People don't want to believe that. They see shouting at women in the streets as a very different thing to frightening them on buses or saying vile things to them or watching porn all the time because you think that's what you're entitled to.'

Snakish behaviour on your way up the ladder often consists of subtle sexism rather than anything more overt. Nevertheless, it erodes your self-esteem, exploiting what the journalist Mary Ann Sieghart has called an 'authority gap' between men and women. It's so pervasive that women end up having an unconscious bias against themselves and so get into the habit of taking themselves less seriously than they should – expecting less and being satisfied with less; assuming, as she puts it, that 'a man knows what he's talking about until he proves otherwise'. 'As long as we see many more men than women in positions of authority, we will tend to associate men with authority and women with subordinate status. As long as we allow boys to grow up believing that they are superior to girls, we are instilling habits of mind that will be very hard to change in later life.'[60]

The so-called 'surgeon's dilemma' is one of the best-known examples of unconscious bias training. It goes like this: a father and his son are involved in a horrific car crash and the man dies at the scene. But when the child arrives at the hospital and is rushed into the operating theatre, the surgeon pulls away and says, 'I can't operate on this boy, he's my son.' How can this be?

Once you know the answer – that the surgeon is the boy's mother – it seems blindingly obvious. But even though I consider myself a staunch feminist, when a colleague tested me on this scenario, I got it wrong.

The patriarchy remains so entrenched that women need to throw themselves into creating social networks to match men's. Thankfully, the evidence suggests this is happening. According to a 2018 study by the University of California, more than 75 per cent of women in high-ranking positions have a female-dominated inner circle, or strong ties to a few women in their network with whom they are in frequent contact.[61]

'Never be scared of asking [women] for help,' the chef Romy Gill advises me. 'Write to them. Say, "I like what you do, how can I do it?" Don't think, if I'm getting this job then I don't want to give it to anyone else. When women see women are helping each other, then more women help each other. It's important to uplift other people.'

Former Labour Home Secretary Jacqui Smith's comments echo this sentiment: 'Sometimes, as women, we're slightly nervous about whether or not we should use our networks in that way. Trust me, loads of men I know would be happy to do that. And I am now perfectly happy to help others with that. So build those networks, keep going.'

Jacqui found this approach helpful when her political career came to an abrupt end. Having been appointed the first female Home Secretary by Gordon Brown, she resigned that role in June 2009 following her involvement in the parliamentary expenses scandal; then lost her seat as MP for Redditch in the 2010 General Election. Among the revelations was that her (now ex) husband had claimed for two pornographic films.

'Nobody who leaves Parliament is immediately able to find another job and if you've got the stuff hanging over you that I had, it's not easy. So first of all I said yes to a lot of things, I did some things both in broadcasting and other areas that were a bit scary to me at the time. I used my contacts. I made new contacts. I kept in touch with people.'

When Jacqui's troubled marriage finally ended, a different kind of network supported her – the friends and family she felt bad for having neglected in the years when she was too busy to breathe. 'I realised that there are people who are happy to step up and help you and stand beside you and keep you cheerful.'

Currently the director of the religious thinktank Theos, Chine McDonald got to study how male networks operate up close when she went to Cambridge University to study Theology and Religion. While there she combined being News Editor of the university newspaper *Varsity* with getting as many work placements as she could. As a practising Christian, her ambition was to unite her interest in religion and news by becoming a religious correspondent for, say, the *Guardian*. That her career didn't ultimately develop in that direction she ascribes partly to the power of male networks.

'Looking back at Cambridge, there were lots of men who had connections within the media who were possibly bolder and braver than I was at pushing themselves forward. They are now top journalists and editors and I often wonder why that didn't happen [for me] . . . After university I thought I would walk into a newspaper job, but there were various shut doors – many, many no's.'

Female allies are vital, not least because they can change your entire perception of an institution. Finding Harriet Harman as a mentor gave Labour MP Jess Phillips the confidence to see that, for all its faults, Westminster had much to commend it as a workplace. 'Don't be discouraged because it isn't a toxic environment where women are cowering in the corner the whole time,' Jess says. 'None of us are like that. It's actually a great place to work in lots and lots of ways and I think it gets talked down dreadfully.'

Having moved to London in the early 1980s after abandoning a Law degree, *Bridgerton* star Adjoa Andoh quickly got her acting career up and running. In doing so she benefited enormously from an atmosphere that was, she says, collegiate rather than nakedly competitive. 'Other black women started to tell me about auditions and I've never forgotten the generosity of that. You know, "Here's a job . . . and you will be in competition with me to get the job." You've got to pass it on and that's become a mantra for me.'

As a fledgling reporter I was lucky enough to find female mentors too. At the *Independent* I encountered then-Comment Editor Jane Taylor, who gave me brilliant, eye-rolling advice on how to navigate male egos on Fleet Street and beyond. Ditto Alice Rawsthorn at the *Financial Times*, whose combination of professionalism and poise offered me an invaluable life lesson as a young media reporter. A couple of promotions later, as a Political Correspondent, fellow *FT* lobby journalist Rosemary Bennett became a great friend, a relationship forged against a backdrop of low-level sexism and male machismo in Westminster.

All of which said, the assumption that women are naturally supportive of each other and that successful women are more inclined than successful men to 'send the elevator down' isn't necessarily true. A fascinating study by Joyce Benenson, a lecturer in the Department of Human Evolutionary Biology at Harvard University, showed that girls were more likely to respond to perceived social threats by forming exclusionary alliances. The goals, as always, are 'survival and reproductive success'. The methods employed to attain them are pure *Mean Girls*:

'From early childhood onwards, girls compete using strategies that minimise the risk of retaliation and reduce the strength of other girls. Girls' competitive strategies include avoiding direct interference with another girl's goals, disguising competition, competing overtly only from a position of high status in the community, enforcing equality within the female community and socially excluding other girls.'[62]

The aphorism 'There is a special place in hell for women who don't support other women' is usually attributed to the first female US Secretary of State, Madeleine Albright. Margaret Thatcher is frequently offered up as an example of the Queen Bee who treated other women badly, keeping them down because she didn't want them to reach her level. Interviewed for Julia Gillard and Ngozi Okonjo-Iweala's book, Thatcher's successor as female Prime Minister, Theresa May, accused female journalists of wanting to prove themselves by being harsher on female politicians than on male ones: 'You would think there was a sort of sisterhood – we want to promote women in politics – but there's none of that.'[63]

As we saw earlier, Chine McDonald was frustrated by all the closed doors after she left Cambridge. But she might not have ended up at Cambridge at all had she not found a *male* ally in an unlikely place. 'I decided I wanted to be a journalist, so I spent almost every holiday from the age of 15 or 16 at different newspapers and magazines to get work experience. I happened to be on the features desk of the *Independent* in the summer when I was getting my GCSE results. I decided to ask for advice from the Features Editor because I wanted him to remember me. He said, brilliantly, "Well, you're black and you're a woman and the media is still very much an old boys' network made up of people who went to Oxbridge, so I would try to go to the best university you can and study any subject because it's very much about networking."'

I found the best definition of an ally (in the social justice sense) in *Harvard Business Review*: 'Allies work publicly and privately to change workplace practices, cultures, and policies that negatively impact marginalised groups. By building authentic and trusting relationships, engaging in public advocacy and sponsorship, and fighting injustice, allies help to create equitable professional and social spaces by strategically deploying their privilege in support of those less privileged . . . Anyone and everyone can be an ally. But male allies who recognize and understand the importance of fostering an inclusive, welcoming, and equitable workplace culture can help break down the barriers that women face at work.'[64]

Into this category I would put my friend Mathew Horsman, who was Media Editor of the *Independent* when I worked there in the late 1990s. His best advice was never to take a break for lunch unless you're lunching a contact and always disappear to the loo to make a contemporaneous note of any lunch or dinner gossip offered up by a source. He's always been brilliantly supportive of me and later gave me valuable advice from his Olympian perch as a media analyst.

But I think male allyship starts early – in childhood. Several of my *Ladder* interviewees have talked about the importance of their relationships with their fathers.

Broadcaster Joan Bakewell had a close, nurturing relationship with hers. She grew up basking in his approval, as she puts it. 'I remember when I used to do my homework he would sit beside me reading a book – not so that he would do my homework for me but, as he said, "just in case there's something you'd like to ask me". It was an enormous act of confidence and friendship.' She felt she had both parents behind her, willing her on. 'They were eager that I should take the eleven-plus and do well. They didn't overdo it. I don't remember doing extra work or anything. But they smiled when I succeeded and frowned when I didn't and I wanted more smiles than frowns.'

I like this a lot and it reminds me of something said to me by the Executive Vice President of AstraZeneca Pam Cheng, who was born in China but raised in New Jersey. Her father had told her it was too difficult for women to succeed in science and engineering and tried to put her off a career in that field – but this turned out to be a reverse-psychology ruse designed to bring out the fighter in Pam, which it absolutely did.

The father of Arminka Helić, the foreign policy expert who was Special Adviser to William Hague when he was Foreign Secretary, was a defence civil servant: 'He knew that to run the household with my mum you needed a bit of order and discipline.' Arminka was the youngest of five and 'probably the naughty one'. Her father was a vital source of support to her when she was growing up and backed her decision as a teenager not to join the Communist Party in her home country of Bosnia and Herzegovina. 'I'm quite stubborn. If I believe something, I go 100 per cent; if I don't, you can't move me. That is the influence of my parents, who believed that right and wrong are not shades of black and white, they really are black and white . . . What I would say is that my dad was broad-minded and strong enough to allow me to have my say in what I wanted to do and didn't, and that would have come with a price. When I came home and said, "This is what I've done", he never said, "Oh, you shouldn't have". Instead he would say, "That's your decision". I was 14 or 15 and it's quite something to get that support at such a young age.'

Having a father who believed so profoundly in girls' agency was also important to Jude Kelly. 'It took me a long time to realise not every man thought like that,' she admits to me. 'I think if you're brought up to feel optimistic about yourself early on then it's easier to cope with dismay later. And my dad always made me feel that I could do things.'

There's a long history of men campaigning for feminist goals. Utopian socialist William Thompson and liberal philosopher John Stuart Mill were significant contributors to the women's movement in the nineteenth century. At the first Women's Liberation Conference, held at Ruskin College, Oxford in February 1970, men famously handled all the childcare. As the film-maker Sue Crockford, who was there, pointed out, this was seen at the time as remarkable: 'Most conferences in those days didn't have creches. You were supposed to have dealt with your kids somewhere else . . . So to have a creche on site run by blokes was, well, I suppose we thought it was mildly radical, but when we started to talk to people about it and they said, "Blokes run it?!" we said, "Why not?"'[65]

Jude Kelly remembers leaving Birmingham University, where she'd studied Drama, and finding almost no women in prominent positions, 'so the most helpful people did end up being male allies. Both Peter Cheeseman, who ran the Victoria Theatre in Stoke-on-Trent, and Charles Parker, who created Radio Ballads, enlightened me from different directions as to how art was something withheld from most people's ability to join in because of education, history and cultural expectations. And I became really committed, almost evangelically, to saying art must be for everyone. That is the purpose of it. I wanted to see how I could use theatre to bridge gaps around cultural access.'

When she left university, within a year she'd started her own company in Southampton (Solid People's Theatre): a touring company featuring pub shows, musicals, part of the ecosystem of community theatre, 'putting on theatre in non-conventional spaces for audiences who might never go to the theatre'.

'Those male allies were critical because if you have a society where the legitimacy is male, you can't buck it. So when you get that given to you wholeheartedly for who you are – not patronising you, not putting a paternalistic arm around you but "I'm on your side and I'm with you and I respect you as my equal" – it takes away so many of the inner voices that you've been encouraged to have. We are given inner voices of doubt intentionally and that's not just true of women: any minoritised person knows they wrestle with their inner self-value. That's not to say I hold men's opinions as more important than women's, I do not. I need women's good opinion of me, but certainly in my earlier life having men tell me I should carry on was a big help.'

Successful women carry burdens that would be unthinkable to men, not least worrying about whether they have opened up professions enough to allow other women passage. Screenwriter Abi Morgan remembers attending events for TV writers in the early days of her career where she was one of perhaps two or three female writers in the room. She feels keenly the importance of sending the elevator down, but marvels at one particular difference in attitude she's noticed in up-and-coming talent. 'The generation [of women writers] behind me are much more comfortable with owning their place at the table. My generation sat at the table and went, "Thanks so much for having me." Whereas this generation goes, "Thanks for having me, and here's what else I can bring: I'm going to direct and I'm going to produce . . ." And they're only in their twenties and thirties.'

Lady Brenda Hale's dedication to upholding the rule of law and status as a trailblazer for women in the judiciary has solidified her reputation as one of the most respected legal minds in Britain. She became a Queen's Counsel in 1989 and a High Court judge in 1994. Brenda was the second woman ever to be appointed as a Lord of Appeal in Ordinary, a position she held from 2004 to 2009; then in 2009 she became the first female justice of the newly established Supreme Court.

Brenda's coat of arms, chosen by her on her appointment to the House of Lords, bore the motto *omnia feminae aequissimae*: 'women are equal to everything'.

When we speak for *The Ladder*, I wonder if she felt anxious as a woman that she had to make a success of it, or else. 'It was a long time coming,' she laughs. 'It's a shame they didn't find somebody before me but they did find me, so of course you have to step up to the plate, however nervous you may feel about it. You've got to do it.

'I think you definitely feel that you mustn't let other women down. The other thing you mustn't do is pull up the drawbridge. Try and make sure that the way is clear for other women to climb the ladder after you.'

Like all successful women, Brenda was accused by a male colleague of being 'not easy to deal with'. The diaries of former Supreme Court Deputy President Lord Hope revealed that when she first ran for Supreme Court President in 2012 she was pitted against Lords Neuberger and Mance. Lord Hope reportedly wrote that while he thought eventual winner Neuberger would be 'a real pleasure to work with', Brenda's strong views on feminism seemed to put her on the 'defensive for much of the time'. He also wrote that she was 'relentless in her pursuit of her agenda about women' – as if this was a bad thing!

In a male-dominated workplace, do women have to be difficult to be successful?

'I don't myself think that most of my colleagues on the bench thought I was difficult to work with,' says Brenda, cautiously. 'There may have been one or two and of course you have to bear in mind the time I was on the bench – until very recently there had been so few women that they [i.e. men] didn't necessarily know how to cope with us. It was possible to construe certain behaviours as being difficult when that wasn't the intention at all; possible to get bothered about how we might react to things when there's no reason to get bothered. I just think it is men who were used to, and understood, men and their reactions who weren't used to, and didn't understand, women and their reactions. And of course a lot of the time there was no difference.'

More important to Brenda than being a trailblazer is what she was able to do once she had acquired power.

'I couldn't have promoted the domestic violence legislation which there was in 1996 if I hadn't been at the Law Commission and established good relations with the Lord Chancellor. I couldn't have been party to the Yemshaw decision about what we now call coercive control if I hadn't been one of the justices of the Supreme Court, so you have to have the position.'

That implies a man might not have chosen to work on the same laws?

'That's possible.'

It's hard, Brenda says, for women to practise law and balance it with having a family, 'particularly if you go into independent practice at the bar because although you're self-employed and can to a certain extent determine your own diary, when you're starting off and for quite a considerable time it is very difficult to run your own diary. I was at the general common law bar in Manchester and the drill was when you were starting out you would stay in chambers until six or seven o'clock in the hope that a brief for the following day would come in and that brief might send you off to Carlisle or Preston or Wigan or anywhere in the region and you'd have to sit up half the night preparing and then you'd have to get up early to get there. Now this is not an easy life to combine with having childcare or other family care responsibilities.'

The Bar is trying to fix this – for example, having a rule saying you're not expected to reply to emails after a certain time in the evening. More than anything, though, 'you need access to good childcare facilities and it's a great help to have a supportive partner. It's not only picking up slack with childcare, it's the psychological support. When my husband and I were discussing my going back to work after I'd had my daughter – and because she was very premature the circumstances were more anxious than they might otherwise have been – he said, "Well, I wouldn't dream of giving up my work just because I'd had a baby, so I don't see why you should." Now that sort of attitude is very helpful.'

Brenda's spider brooch gained attention during the delivery of the Supreme Court's judgement on the prorogation of Parliament in 2019. She wore the brooch during the announcement of the ruling, which declared the prorogation as unlawful. To say it caught the attention of the media would be an understatement: many column inches were spent discussing its meaning and significance. At one point it even got its own Twitter/X account.

There's something satisfying, then, in the fact that it was a gift from another male ally: her (second) husband.

'I have many brooches, most of them creatures, quite a lot of them spiders, which have been given to me by my husband over the years to liven up the rather sober dress which is expected of judges. They tend to migrate to a particular garment and stay there. I chose that demure black dress and it happens to carry a spider . . . It wasn't at all an expensive brooch. My husband tells me he got it from a certain well-known card shop that also sells costume jewellery and it probably cost him around £12.'

Sadly, history does not record if she has any brooches in the shape of snakes . . .

HOW TO AVOID
SNAKES

- Be scrupulous about supporting other women in the workplace, whether you're a manager who is in a position to provide training, review salaries, implement the correct recruitment policies, etc., or a more junior worker on her way up.

- A piece in *Forbes* magazine[66] made this great point, which can be hard to keep sight of when you think what's going on might be no more than bonding banter you'd look uptight for calling out: Give yourself permission to feel offended. 'Benevolent sexism', e.g. unsolicited 'compliments' or indeed compliments that aren't really compliments, e.g. being described as 'great at photocopying', is still sexism.

- Know your rights. The Equality Act 2010 defines sexual harassment as 'unwanted conduct of a sexual nature which has the purpose or effect of violating someone's dignity, or creating an intimidating, hostile, degrading, humiliating or offensive environ-ment for them'. Something can still be considered sexual harassment, even if the alleged harasser didn't mean for it to be.

5

ADVERSE EFFECTS

When she was a child, the conductor Alice Farnham lived with her family in a large rectory in the Norfolk village where her father was the local priest. In many ways it was a privileged childhood: comfortable, middle-class. 'We didn't have much money – clergy aren't rich – but it was a rich childhood in terms of freedom and my father wasn't strict,' she says.

She and her sister were encouraged to be adventurous, with no sense that any activity was off-limits because they were girls. But life changed radically for both of them when their father drowned in a boating accident in April 1980, a few weeks before Alice's tenth birthday. Her sister, who had been in the boat with friends, nearly died as well. Alice watched the tragedy unfold from the shore. 'I remember it vividly,' she writes in her memoir *In Good Hands*, 'and part of my childhood and self-confidence was left on the shore that day.'[67]

Afterwards, she says, she was very well looked after

and there was a lot of kindness and warmth. It helped too that Alice knew her father hadn't been afraid of death. ('Our mother said that and we said, "Yes, we know." There was no euphemism around death in our family. So I was able to work through it in the short term and block it out, but the aftermath was harder.') One of the traumas of losing a parent who is clergy is that the house comes with the job – 'and if you leave the job then obviously you leave the house'.

'We had about three months to uproot ourselves afterwards. We'd been at the centre of a small village and my parents had always kept an open door. Then we moved to a little coastal town and nobody knew us, we were completely anonymous, and that was quite traumatic when I think about it. Although my mum was amazing and very supportive, what happens when you lose a parent when you're young is you develop a sense of responsibility very early that you shouldn't have. So I didn't want to worry my mum by saying I was upset by that and that's a formative thing that affects you for the rest of your life.'

The early trauma gave Alice a seriousness and focus that set her apart from her peers. Music soon became a balm and a solace. In the summer after her father's death, she taught herself to read music and became obsessed with playing the piano. Sent to a fee-paying school which gave free places to 'clergy orphans', at 13 she started learning the organ and eventually won an organ scholarship to Oxford University. There, she cut her conducting teeth with choirs and acquired the confidence to lead and direct that she had admired in other people.

'My first experience of conducting was disastrous and I didn't want to do it at all. I already thought I wasn't clever enough to be at Oxford, so how could I stand in front of these people and tell them what to do?'

Gradually, though, she came to realise she knew as much as anyone else – they were just better at winging it and pretending. 'I thought you had to know everything whereas they thought, "Oh, I don't know everything but I'll have a go anyway."' This 'having a go' resulted in a sort of epiphany. 'You need to breathe, to take a breath as you bring in a group of people; then they will breathe with you and they will be able to sing. In my second year at Oxford, I conducted Faure's "Requiem" and I realised I actually loved the interaction; that sitting at an organ was lonely and I was actually better at conducting.'

Early trauma can destabilise you forever. But some lucky people seem able to channel that pain into something positive: not transcend it exactly, but sublimate it in the psychoanalytic sense. Being a 'clergy orphan' sounds like something out of *Jane Eyre*. But of course Jane is the classic example from literature of someone who faced hardship, in her case neglect and abuse, during her childhood but found salvation, if that's not too strong a word, in education and self-improvement. Jane's years at Lowood school introduced her to the excitement of intellectual achievement. As she says: 'I toiled hard, and my success was proportionate to my efforts; my memory, not naturally tenacious, improved with practice: exercise sharpened my wits.' Her sense of self-worth is transformed and her achievements result in her being promoted to a teaching role.

At her secondary school, Alice was put in a class with children a year younger than her – deliberately and for well-meaning reasons that were never explained to her. In her book, she muses that this was not perhaps the best to boost the confidence of a girl who'd just lost her father 'but I was quickly learning resilience and to keep these upsets to myself. Eventually I convinced myself that being given that extra year was just what I needed to realise my musical and intellectual potential, and I still believe that'.[68]

Were it not for her father's death, Alice Farnham says, music might not have played such a part in her life. The experience made her more adaptable 'because I wasn't frightened'. 'When you lose a parent or sibling, you know that one of the most terrible things has happened and you can still carry on. The worst has happened and it isn't the end of the world.'

Lady Brenda Hale's father also died when she was young, though at 13 she was older than Alice. 'It was a great shock,' she says, 'because we had no reason to suppose there was anything the matter. He hadn't been ill and then he had a heart attack, I think it was – we were never told. It pulled the rug from under us all. But our mother did her very best to keep things going for her daughters. She picked herself up and got a job as head teacher of the local primary school, which was the one my sister and I had both been to. So that meant we could stay in the same village, carry on going to Richmond High School, keep all our friends and continuity, which was very, very good and strong of her. That's why she's a role model to me.'

In her memoir *Spider Woman*, Brenda elaborates interestingly on the effect her father's death had on her. 'Looking back, I feel sure that the sudden loss of security, and regaining it through our mother's resourcefulness, is what made me so determined to qualify for a career, to carry on working whether or not I married or had a family, and never to become wholly dependent upon anyone else, this at a time when marriage and a family were the height of most girls' ambitions.'[69]

In our chaotic post-pandemic world, stoicism feels like one of the most useful virtues in the repertoire. Certainly, it's never been more fashionable. Deep in Silicon Valley, it's said tech bros drink deep from the ultimate source: the *Meditations* of the Roman emperor Marcus Aurelius. 'The impediment to action advances action,' Aurelius tells us. 'What stands in the way becomes the way.'

The tenets of stoicism include self-discipline, resilience and moderating your emotions even when you're provoked; also – and this is crucial – not worrying about what you can't control. So rather than fight death, you accept its inevitability to the point where you grieve loved ones while they are still alive so that their deaths, when they do occur, don't floor you.

The way bestselling tech bro Ryan Holiday sells it in his books and in his podcast *The Daily Stoic*, stoicism has a distinctly macho tinge. But women know better than anyone that people are defined by how they respond to obstacles.

Certainly, it would be hard to get much more stoical

than the Paralympic champion Tanni Grey-Thompson, whose autobiography *Seize the Day* begins: 'I've never cried because I'm in a wheelchair and I've never felt bitter. This is just the way it is.'[70]

Born with spina bifida, Tanni could walk when she was young ('though never well'), but as she grew her spine collapsed, paralysing her. 'My parents' attitude was, well, you can't change it so what are you going to do, sit there and moan about it? My father, who's an architect, refused to make the house wheelchair-accessible because his attitude was: if they made that the only place I could live, that *would* be the only place I could live. So I went up the stairs on my bottom, lifting my legs up one by one . . .'

In her early teens, Tanni had a metal rod put into her spine and bone grafts taken from both hips to attach it, a huge procedure about which her parents were characteristically matter-of-fact. After three weeks, she left hospital in a massive plaster-cast jacket running all the way from her chin to her hips. She had to wear it for six months. 'My sister used to just come and spray perfume. I mean, it was revolting after six months. But I remember going back for a check-up about five or six weeks after the operation and the doctor saying to me, "How's the home tutoring going?" And it's like, "I'm not being tutored at home." "What do you mean?" "I'm back at school." "What? When? When did you go back?" "No, no. I came out of hospital. And literally the next Monday, Mum sent me back to school." He's like, "Oh . . ."'

'When I became a wheelchair-user lots of people would drag their children out of my way and say things like, "Don't get too close to her, you might catch it." I overheard someone saying [to my mother], "Why did you keep it?"'

Rather than cover Tanni's ears and rush her away, her mother used the event as an excuse for a 'really open' conversation about abortion in which she admitted that, had she had access to modern diagnostic techniques, she might have terminated the pregnancy. (Tanni pointed out that this is very far from the same as saying, 'Having had you, I wish I'd terminated you'.) By the same token, the refusal to remodel the house was because they believed the best thing for Tanni was to be independent: to live, one day, in a place that wasn't home.

Tough love isn't the right approach for everyone, but in Tanni's case it fostered the most incredible can-do mindset. Over the course of her athletic career she won a total of 16 Paralympic medals for wheelchair-racing, including 11 golds. But after retiring from sport in 2007 she went on to new heights, presenting TV shows and taking on a number of consultancy and advisory roles. In 2010, she became a life peer and sits in the House of Lords as Baroness Grey-Thompson of Eaglescliffe.

For all the criticism and abuse parliamentarians get, Westminster is stuffed full of inspirational people like Tanni. Few have a more extraordinary 'hinterland', as the former Labour Party Chancellor of the Exchequer Denis Healey called it, than Labour's engaging deputy leader Angela Rayner.

Her challenging childhood – her mother has bipolar disorder, her father was mostly absent – meant her education was seriously disrupted. After having a baby at 16, Angela left school without any formal qualifications, but despite this enrolled in college as a mature student.

'Mum and Dad didn't work,' she tells me. 'They got the giro once a fortnight. So we were poor but I didn't see myself as poor. I was low in the pecking order, though, and I didn't have loads of cousins and brothers who were going to look after me if I was bullied; plus I was a ginger kid which put you in another category of getting bullied. I call myself a feral child. I was always out on the street, playing on rope swings or building dens.

'My mother had learning difficulties. When she hit her thirties her mental health really dipped. Where she'd been just about coping before, now she had three children and was living in poverty. My dad was out a lot and didn't see it as his job to look after children so my mum would struggle . . . My mum used to cry and not get out of bed and she wouldn't wash. So I became her friend and confidante, and her main carer. Our house was really dirty. It's funny because now, me and my two siblings are all really houseproud. Often my mum would row with my dad and he would shout at her. I remember sleeping at the bottom of her bed, worried that if I left her then when I woke up she wouldn't be there. I would have been about 10. When people ask "How did you cope?", that was my reality, I had to cope. I didn't know I was in poverty. I didn't know my mother had never read a book.'

After completing her education Angela worked for the Stockport branch of the trade union Unison. 'I got a job at the council and my work colleagues asked me to be their union rep. I didn't know what a union was but was duly elected as a workplace rep and worked my way up through the ranks, always an elected officer and not a paid official. It taught me the importance of elected office and representation and prepared me for the mayhem of the last eight years in Parliament. The union was a place that accepted me for who I was. I felt I had a purpose and was part of something bigger than me.'

The history of immigration is one of resilience and adaptability. Those qualities are needed right at the start, as Clair Wills' brilliant history of post-war immigration to Britain, *Lovers and Strangers*, makes clear: 'You jacked in your part-time job digging ditches for the County Council in Mayo . . . and bought your ticket for Holyhead. You queued – and queued – in the refugee camp in Germany's British Occupation Zone, for a place on one of the labour schemes which would bring you to a job in a mill in Bradford, or a mine in Wales. You applied by post to a hospital in Lincolnshire from Kingston, Jamaica, and when the letter of acceptance came you borrowed the fare.'[71]

Margaret Hodge has had a long and prominent career in the Labour Party. She was born in 1944 in Alexandria, to which her Jewish family had fled from Germany in 1938. But in 1948 there was a rise in antisemitism triggered by the Arab-Israeli War. After a stone was thrown through the window of his office, her father decided to leave Egypt and move the family to Orpington in Kent.

'I was four and a half and I remember the journey. I remember that the plane had to refuel in Rome. Then when we arrived we went to a B&B and I remember so vividly the food. I was used to luscious, rich fruits and instead there was boiled cabbage and horrid porridge.'

Despite the privations and, of course, the anti-semitism that has always existed just below the surface in Britain, Margaret says that 'being a refugee has completely made me who I am today: my politics, the reason I joined the Labour Party, the battles I've been involved with. They stem from my Jewish identity and that feeling of being a bit of an outsider.'

Arminka Helić also escaped to Britain, in her case from the Bosnian War of the early 1990s. In 1992, after the United States and the European community recognised the newly independent nation of Bosnia and Herzegovina, its Muslim population was targeted by Bosnian Serbs assisted by Serbs from the Yugoslavian army. Their goal was genocide or 'ethnic cleansing', their methods horrific.

The first shock for Arminka was watching as all the structures and certainties of her childhood disappeared. 'When you're growing up in a country where you've spent your formative years being taught about the concept of brotherhood – I was more aware of the Communist manifesto than of the Bible or the Koran or anything else – you simply cannot believe that anyone can turn against anyone, because we were all brought up to believe that we were there to help each other, to lean on each other, to respect our differences.'

The moment of fleeing she remembers as 'one of those very rare moments where I was living in the moment.

The danger was close to us and it wasn't a choice of wanting to leave or not wanting to leave, it was pure necessity. There was no question of having a discussion about what to do and when to do it, it was forced upon everyone – after hearing the news that town after town was falling, that men and women were being separated and the women put into rape camps. Some were shot in the streets and houses marked by crosses to indicate who lived where. My father didn't want us to wait and see what happened to us.'

In a surreal twist, Arminka ended up being taken in by the family of the Conservative politician Sir John Nott, who lived in Chelsea. His wife had been working with refugees in Slovenia, where Arminka had ended up. 'She met me and there was a connection and she invited me to come and stay "until this crisis blows over", as everyone believed it would.'

Arminka's experience also shaped her politically, although it was the Conservative Party she joined in 1997 rather than the newly reborn Labour Party, impressed that Margaret Thatcher had 'managed to see the problem in 1991 that others wouldn't. I found her certainty really appealing'.

'The biggest thing I learned [from my experiences] is not to be swayed by other people's opinions and not to ever be seduced by praise or depressed by criticism. Stick to what you believe in and really work. Don't get distracted. Be calm as water.'

The trauma and upheaval that Arminka experienced has resulted in a heightened moral clarity – a kind of hyper-alertness to systemic injustice. I'd say the same is true of the Female Genital Mutilation (FGM) campaigner Nimco Ali. I'll always remember her quitting her post as a Home Office adviser live on air in December 2022 – because it was me she was talking to. She and the Home Secretary Suella Braverman were, she said, 'on completely different planets when it comes to the rights of women and girls, and also the way that we talk about ethnic minorities'.

Nimco's refusal to be binary in her political thinking stems from witnessing first-hand the results of real-world tribalism in Somaliland: as a child she saw her grandfather being dragged out of his house for demanding equality for his and Nimco's tribe, the Isaaq clan. For a time she believed he had been executed. 'I realised then that you couldn't be silent in the face of injustice,' she says. 'I thought: I'm going to study law because if you study law you're always going to be able to stand your ground and argue.'

After moving to the UK, Nimco had a happy early childhood in Manchester and then Cardiff, but everything changed aged seven when she was taken on what she thought was a holiday back to Djibouti to see her grandparents. In fact, she was about to undergo FGM.

'The cutter looked completely terrifying,' she remembers. 'She was carrying her little case which had her scissors and her tools and her local anaesthesia. There wasn't that cognitive connection of knowing she was going to mutilate me. But I knew she was going to do something horrible. So it was scary but like an out-of-body experience. Do I remember the pain? I don't remember the actual cutting or the stitching me up. I remember the persistence, the need to be woken every hour to pee and that was extremely painful and sharp, so painful that I ended up not wanting to do it and that led to the complications that I ended up having.

'I wasn't able to empty my bladder properly so that ended up becoming a urinary tract infection and then an infection of my kidneys which is a lifelong thing that can be aggravated by stress – so FGM is the gift that keeps on giving. I'm a lot luckier than many girls I know because I ended up having medical intervention so young it meant I could menstruate with the barrier of FGM, have relations, as it were. But they almost killed me, the kidney infections.'

The psychological aftermath was also severe. 'As a child I was keen on overachieving, then I developed an eating disorder. I tried to eat my feelings so I became massively obese. Then I was bulimic from the age of 14 into my late twenties.'

Having experienced FGM first-hand, Nimco became determined to raise awareness of the practice and work towards its eradication. Hence the organisation Daughters of Eve, which she co-founded with Leyla Hussein 'so we could get legislation changed and say, "This is about girls, not about communities."' She also co-founded (with Brendan Wynne) the Five Foundation, which works at a systemic level to advocate for better funding streams for women on the African continent and beyond.

For Nimco, the important thing is confronting the societal taboos – around vaginas and periods, for example – that allow trauma and abuse to happen. In her excellent book *What We're Told Not To Talk About (But We're Going To Anyway)* she writes that 'periods, like FGM, seemed to be an unspoken rite of passage with the women in my family'. At the feast her mother prepared to celebrate Nimco's first period, Nimco noticed 'a glance pass between my mother and my grandmother'.[72] Only years later does she wonder if it was one of relief, that the FGM had not stopped her from menstruating normally.

Her book lobbed a tampon grenade into the middle of all that secrecy, collecting in-your-face stories about periods and sex from women and girls across the world. It combines consciousness-raising with a kind of narrative therapy that aims to shift the dial from shame to celebration.

I'm so used to using the word 'voiceless' metaphorically that it was a shock to talk to two women for whom voicelessness had, earlier in their lives, been a literal predicament.

I was struck when interviewing Rehana Azam, former national secretary of the GMB union, for *The Ladder* by how beautifully she spoke: in precise, carefully constructed sentences. I couldn't have predicted the reason why.

'My mum and dad didn't speak English, they didn't have any education, so my first language was Punjabi. I always struggled at nursery to converse and the staff thought it was because I couldn't speak English. But it became clear that it wasn't just the language, it was how I was pronouncing words. I actually had a lisp and my mum's way of dealing with this was very old-school: she used to give me warm honey and almonds. The school had to speak to my mum and say no, she needs a speech therapist. The therapist had to spend a lot of time building my confidence just to speak and that's how I learned to construct my sentences perfectly. It's the result of years of thinking before speaking, of remembering how to get the words out.'

The film director and children's rights advocate Beeban Kidron was born with a cleft palate which she had corrected by surgery when she was 18 months old. 'I had a special bottle so I didn't choke when I was fed. As a result I had problems with my vocal cords when I was about ten years old and I used to [makes croaky voice] *speak like this*. Actually, I had a very broad Yorkshire accent as well, I'd like to point out! I had to have [another] operation and because I was so young they tried first to stop me speaking.

'I used to walk around with a horn like Harpo Marx and a little booklet hung on my belt. It was a very difficult time because it was the transition from primary to secondary school. So I arrived at secondary school with a horn and a booklet, unable to speak, and the teachers all thought: Great, we'll bring her forward and she can write on the board. But I was humiliated by it and at that time Fay Godwin, the landscape photographer and a friend of my parents, gave me a camera and said, "If you can't speak, why don't you make pictures?" And incredibly, that was the beginning of the rest of my life.

'I think the curiously optimistic nature that I have is because out of every bad thing that's happened to me, some incredible good has come. And that was possibly the first indication that that would be so.'

Beeban went on to be mentored by the legendary American photographer Eve Arnold, who spotted some of her photos in a feminist magazine and asked her to be her assistant. 'When she first asked I had to tell her, "I'm going to be 14 tomorrow." She laughed but she did ring me [again] on my sixteenth birthday and say, "Do you want to come now?" – and so I left school to work for her. I'd never got on very well at school. I didn't quite understand school and I don't think school ever quite understood me. Many years later, when I was in my early forties, I discovered by accident that I actually have some dyslexia and learning difficulties and I wonder whether that was something to do with it. But I went on to work for Eve and she taught me all the important things that I now know at that very young age.'

At the age of 20, Beeban enrolled at the National Film School to study cinematography but after three years switched to directing 'because I didn't like being pushed around'. When she left she worked initially in documentaries before moving into drama. Before long she had made her wonderful adaptation of Jeanette Winterson's novel *Oranges Are Not the Only Fruit* for the BBC.

'It was very contentious at the time, but immensely popular and much loved by a very broad audience. It was also my step to Hollywood. Steven Spielberg and George Lucas got hold of a copy. They clubbed together and bought me a ticket to LA so that they could meet me. So when people ask me, "How do you get to Hollywood?" I say, "You make a drama about evangelical Christians and lesbianism".'

Spielberg proved a generous mentor. 'I was directing a film called *To Wong Foo, Thanks for Everything! Julie Newmar* when I found out I was pregnant. I rang up Spielberg, who was one of the producers, and said, "Listen, I've got news . . ." There was a crash in the background because one of his children had just pulled something off a shelf. He came back and went, "Kids, huh?" and I said, "That's a good segue because I'm pregnant." He said, "Mazel tov!" and I said, "No, you're not understanding, I can no longer get insurance to make the movie." He said, "I have loads of children and I've made loads of movies. Give me a minute." A bit later he called back and said, "It's okay, we're getting insurance for you. It's costing a fortune, but the real caveat is if anything happens to you because of the pregnancy, I will direct on those days . . .'

It can sometimes feel as if our lives have two halves, like a profit and loss ledger in a company accounts book. The first half we spend acquiring the things that we hope will define us and make us happy – friends, education, a partner, a job, children – then we spend the second half losing things. The most heartbreaking stories I heard on *The Ladder* were from women who had lost things early: parents, friends, health, happiness. Perhaps the worst loss of all, your child, is the kind you might think it would be impossible to recover from, but somehow most of them had, to some degree, in some form.

Carolyn Harris, the menopause campaigner and Deputy Leader of Welsh Labour, lost her son Martin in 1989 in a road accident. He was eight years old.

'We were fine,' she told me. 'Then everything changed. It became a different existence.

'At the time you think that as long as you have got breath in your body, you will never ever worry about anything ever again . . . What has happened is the worst thing in the world, the thing you only read about in papers or watch on TV, and you always think: Oh, I feel really sorry for that person, thank God it's not happening to me, it'll never happen to me. When it does happen to you it completely changes how you see everything else around you. Every time something happens – you get a bill, say, or somebody's late in – you never think rationally: Oh, I've got nothing to worry about. You go to the extreme and you think: Absolutely this is the end of the world and something really bad is going to happen. I didn't laugh for a long time [afterwards] and if I did laugh, I felt guilty that I'd laughed. Because how could I laugh when I'd lost Martin? Even now, if I laugh too much, if I'm with friends and I have a good laugh, I feel terrible, because I convince myself that tomorrow it's going to bring tragedy. You feel as if you've been punished, I suppose, and you can't understand why. So it's quite possible you'll be punished again.'

In 2013, at the age of nine, Rosamund Adoo-Kissi-Debrah's daughter Ella died after suffering a severe asthma attack that Rosamund came to believe was directly related to the high levels of air pollution in their local area generated by south-east London's notoriously busy South Circular road.

Ella had always suffered from bad asthma and was admitted to hospital over thirty times after she started to become ill in Year 2. 'It was the October half-term,' Rosamund remembers with chilling exactitude. 'She was really smart. By the time she was 14 or 15 months she knew her alphabet by heart. When she died at nine she had a reading age of 15. Part of that was doctors explaining complex medical decisions to her. They spoiled her because they really liked her, they really liked having her in hospital. Did they think she was going to die? No.'

On 14 February 2013, Valentine's Day, Rosamund was walking around Marks & Spencer in Beckenham with Ella, shopping for a special meal for that evening. 'If you'd said to me that the following day she was going to be no more, I'd have said, "Oh Cathy, don't be silly." The school had called me to tell me she'd had a coughing fit but it was all right, not an emergency. "She's fine, we're just letting you know." So we went to M&S and all I remember of that night is that it was completely normal. Then, when she got into bed, [the asthma] got serious. I read the twins a story and said to Ella, "Get ready and then I'll come and read to you." I'd picked out a story for her, the Beethoven love letter which ends with "ever thine . . ."'

It would be the last story Rosamund ever read to Ella.

'In the early hours of the morning she had one of her attacks. Normally, it would have been possible to resuscitate her. But that night she just didn't come round.'

The first inquest into Ella's death in 2014 found that she had died of 'acute respiratory failure' and made no mention of any environmental factors. With the help of Professor Sir Stephen Holgate and the human rights lawyer Jocelyn Cockburn, Rosamund challenged that verdict, seeking a fresh inquest with the aim of including evidence of air pollution as a contributing factor. In the two days around Ella's death, she learned, there had been big spikes in air pollution locally.

Eventually, in December 2020, a landmark legal ruling in the UK concluded that air pollution *had* contributed to Ella's death. The coroner said there had been a 'recognised failure' of the government and other bodies both to reduce nitrogen dioxide levels and to provide information to the public about their risks. It marked the first time that air pollution had been listed as a cause of death on a death certificate in the country.

'Because of Covid, my lawyer Jocelyn couldn't speak after court because she couldn't come, so when I got out of court there was a microphone . . . I can't even remember what I said. It was really, really, really hard. It took me until after Christmas to take in what had happened.'

Since then Rosamund has thrown herself into activism, creating the Ella Roberta Foundation to honour her daughter's memory by fighting for the implementation of 'Ella's Law', the Clean Air (Human Rights) Bill, introduced to Parliament by Baroness Jenny Jones in May 2022. To recognise her extraordinary achievements and courage, she was made CBE in the 2023 New Year Honours.

'You have to learn to live with your loss,' she says. 'I was lucky, in inverted commas, that I already had faith [in God] before she died. Do I understand why other parents take drugs and drink? I do. I don't do it myself because probably I would never stop. I'm lucky in the sense that I've set up a charity I can focus on. I have my moments, but then I look at my twins . . . The guilt I feel is that when Ella died life was kind of over and it's taken up until now to see a bit of a future because when your child dies, your future is taken away from you. Seriously. It's only now . . . The twins were almost five at the time. It's only now that I can look forward to them going to college or uni. But it will always be with a tinge of sadness that Ella isn't here. For them it's horrendous. They've spent all their lives . . . not in her shadow, they're talented in their own right. But I sometimes imagine what it must be like for them.'

Carolyn Harris says something very similar. 'You don't move on from [grief], you learn to live with it. Every day you wake up and you know how that day is going to be for you. You might wake up and think: Oh it's okay, I can live today, I can enjoy today and you'll get through. There'll be other days when I wake up and think: I want to put the duvet over my head. I call them my pink anorak days because when I did think I had a nervous breakdown I lived in a pink anorak for six months, not going anywhere without my friends or being able to go shopping.'

But Carolyn did not give up on life. Instead, at 34, she became the first person in her family to go to university, studying social history and social policy at Swansea. 'I'd come out from having lost Martin and was working with kids at a special school, kids who were very challenged. And I used to get quite frustrated when it was quite obvious there were times when their parents were exhausted with them and needed a break. I think I was a bit, "How can you think you want a break from your child? If only I could still have Martin . . ." I got a bit resentful and so I thought: I need to do something, I can't have this legacy of pain turning me into a negative person. The only way I could think of to do that was to change what I was doing . . ..'

It's common as we age to experience death in clusters, or as a sort of repeated assault, as happened to actress Maureen Lipman. First, her husband Jack Rosenthal, the celebrated TV writer, died in 2004. 'I think it took me about three years to . . . well, I don't think I've finished grieving yet, to be honest. Then three years ago I lost Guido, my partner of fifteen years. [Guido had a form of Parkinson's and died during the pandemic.] But it's like Alzheimer's – people say, you are the person you are, even if you've got this illness. You are what you are. And I would never be the sort of person who sank into a depression about that because I live each day as it comes. I wouldn't give advice to anyone who's grieving because you've got to do it in your own way. It was a long process when Jack was dying, around two years. Sometimes he was in remission, sometimes he wasn't, because he had myeloma. And I don't want anyone I love to have to be suffering like that. Also, he was 72, which is incredibly young. But I was 58. I didn't realise how young he was. And I lost my mother six months before that. I was in the presence of death and you have no training. You've never spoken about death. You've never seen a dead body . . .'

I've never been a war reporter – ironically, given that it was seeing Kate Adie reporting on the first Gulf War in 1990 that made me want to be a journalist. In the decades since then, we've lived through a succession of conflicts around the world. When war erupts there is shock, outrage and often extensive reporting. Then, all too often, the conflict fades from the headlines: the human misery endures, but the journalistic caravan moves on.

To their credit, when the Syrian war began in March 2011 my boss at the time, Ben de Pear, and his deputy, Nevine Mabro, took a different approach. They came across an extraordinary couple who were documenting the hostilities from the inside, offering a unique, un-rivalled perspective on the human cost of war. They were the journalist Waad Al-Kateab and her surgeon husband Hamza, whom I've had the privilege of getting to know while working alongside them at *Channel 4 News*.

In the summer of 2016, as Aleppo was hit by shells, chlorine gas, cluster and barrel bombs, Waad was living with Hamza and their baby daughter Sama in the hospital Hamza had built. Incensed by the world's blindness to what was going on, by the passivity and inertia, she filmed everything that was happening around her.

Some of this material was broadcast on *Channel 4 News*. Some of it found its way into *For Sama*, the unbearably powerful documentary that astounded audiences when it was released in 2019, winning an Oscar for Best Documentary Feature. We're used to seeing and hearing explosions, the kind of 'shock and awe' tactics that became synonymous with the Iraq War, for example. What made *For Sama* especially poignant was the dissonance between the scenes of ordinary domestic hubbub – Waad being a mother to Sama, children playing in a bombed-out bus – and the surrounding atmosphere of random carnage.

Waad, Hamza and Sama left Aleppo in December 2016 following advice from the UN to evacuate. With help from film-maker Edward Watts, Waad spent the next two years editing the mass of footage into what became *For Sama*. Since then the family has lived in east London, apart from a brief stint in Turkey.

'I was a headstrong girl, the eldest of my siblings – brave but not really brave, sometimes careless even,' she tells me. 'Living in Syria, we weren't trained to know a lot of political issues, we just knew that Assad was president and also like our father, our first teacher – we can't complain or say anything bad about the government or president. I remember all the adults around me going "Shhh" and saying, "The walls have ears."'

At the age of 15, Waad was handed a form which effectively forced her to join the Ba'ath Party. She refused to sign it. 'They never saw it as forcing us, it was naturally something we should do and be: students who have loyalty to the Ba'ath Party, which is the only party in Syria.' At first, it wasn't simply that she didn't want to sign it per se. 'I just wanted to take this paper away with me and think more about it. I felt a responsibility towards this step in my life. I'm grown-up and I have a decision to take, so I wanted to take it responsibly, to think if I want to do it or not. I asked the teacher if it was possible and she took it as a stand, as a rebellious act, that I wanted to make the whole class question [signing the form]. She started shouting, saying bad words to me and how rude I am . . . She kicked me out of the class . . . I went back home crying and as soon as I opened the door I could see my father on the phone to her. As soon as he finished the call he didn't even ask me what had happened. He was like, "Where is the paper?" He tore it up and said, "If you want to sign it, go tomorrow and get a new one. If you don't want to, no one can force you." I'm a person who has a mind, who can say yes and no.'

Her ambition was always to be a journalist. 'I was watching Al Jazeera, looking at journalists and I remember one of them was a female presenter from Palestine – Shireen Abu Akleh, who was killed in 2022 – and for me that was something very exciting and important . . . I had a big argument and debate with my parents about whether to be a journalist or not. We had just one journalism school in Syria which had a very bad reputation because it was controlled by the regime . . . My parents didn't want me to do it. They said, "If you do journalism in Syria, then the day after you graduate you will be arrested because you are a very headstrong girl and you'll never like being controlled by anyone and that's not how our military state works . . ."'

At 18 she moved to Aleppo to study economics but didn't enjoy the experience: 'I hated the whole city and the community there.' In 2015 she started reporting on the Syrian war for *Channel 4 News*. 'I started filming after joining the protests because the regime was denying everything. As an activist I had to do something to empower the revolution, so I started filming with my phone. After a year the equipment and my skills started to improve; also my understanding of what media means.'

Waad first met Hamza in 2011 on a protest. Having made contact on Facebook, they met again on the frontline where he turned up wearing scrubs. 'I remember Zorro, a hero who was rescuing everyone. But Hamza was like that in reality, except that in cartoons heroes never die and, at the end, justice happens. But in this life, no, justice is not happening and heroes might die at the beginning of the story, not just at the end. And that's really scary.'

At first she didn't know how her footage would be used beyond uploading clips on YouTube. 'Then I fell in love and felt this is not just an issue for my country, it's a very personal issue. I found out that I was pregnant – these small moments of happiness and love – and I felt that these moments were as important as the whole disaster that was happening outside. Any second all of us – myself, Hamza and Sama – might be killed.'

Throughout the near-constant shelling and bombing, she kept filming. At times only 'the dream of this free country, the dream of a better life' kept them going. 'I thought: This is the only way for the whole world to see [what's happening] and if they could see it then the nightmare would end. But also: This is just another clip and the world is turning a blind eye.'

The dress Waad wore to the 2020 Oscars ceremony had a message sewn into it – 'we dared to dream and we will not regret dignity', rendered calligraphically in a vibrant pink that matched a plant Waad left behind in her house in Aleppo before she was displaced. Any pressure she felt was not because of the film and wanting to win an Oscar, but because 'I had behind me thousands of people who are waiting to hear our message about Syria. It was a big victory for the revolution, for the Syrian people who have suffered a lot, and that was a big responsibility for me. Every platform means more people will know the story, will know about Syria and could act for Syria.'

Now Waad is in a kind of exile. The psychological hangover from what she and her family have endured will last a long time, possibly forever. It's still hard for her to process the awful things she witnessed. She jokes that she had to give up therapy because her therapist ended up needing a therapist; also because, as long as Assad is in power, the nightmare goes on. 'The thing about processing this as it's still happening is it doesn't make sense. When people talk about PTSD, you need [the thing] to have ended, to be thinking back, not to be thinking, "This is still happening." That's why I had to give it up.' That said, it did help her find a way to (as she puts it) 'shape this pain and the bad memories towards something really positive.'

Waad's advice is that we should 'love and hope and fight'. There are moments of hope in *For Sama*, not least Sama's birth and that of another child, born to an unconscious mother by emergency caesarean. We think he is dead, but then after his chest has been palpitated he opens his eyes and cries out. The mother too is saved. It feels like a miracle, and it is, but the hope it represents is double-edged because it can be unbearable.

Hope is the last thing to escape Pandora's Box: but the question remains of why it was there in the first place. Is hope a blessing or a curse? Before we decide, we need to be clear about what hope is not. I like the poet Seamus Heaney's brisk assessment: 'Hope is not optimism, which expects things to turn out well, but something rooted in the conviction that there is good worth working for.' Or, as the *Oxford English Dictionary* puts it, hope is the 'expectation of something desired; desire combined with expectation'.

Optimism, by contrast, involves looking at the world through rose-tinted glasses, disregarding reality where necessary: what a certain person used to call 'boosterism'. It's foolish, people say. Naive. But these are comfortless, disenchanted days and I wonder if you can't create hope by being optimistic? If you believe in progress, then surely progress is more likely to occur? And don't you sometimes have to believe something is impossible to spur yourself into achieving it?

Another woman who has known unthinkable adversity, Marina Litvinenko, continues to hope at a time when her homeland has set itself against the world by invading Ukraine. For her, hoping takes the form of being a tireless advocate for justice. The loss of Russia – plainly, she can never return as long as Putin is in power – has compounded the loss of her husband Alexander, the Russian defector and former FSB officer who died in November 2006 after being poisoned with polonium-210 by the Russian security services.

Marina was born in Moscow in 1962. 'I believed I lived in the best country and I was very lucky,' she says. 'I was a Young Pioneer in the Communist Party, but then when I was a teenager I was introduced to the world of ballroom dancing . . . I didn't know it would become my professional life because after school I applied to university and I received a degree in oil engineering at the Moscow Oil and Gas Academy. But my passion for dancing was so strong I could not stop doing it even more, as a professional dancer, teacher and competitor and as head of a dance studio . . . It was like internal immigration because life being a dancer was so different. We could travel inside the Soviet Union but also to Baltic countries, which was very special to us. I think I was very lucky to have the chance to see my country from different sides. Even if I was less politically involved, I saw something strange: when you go to Siberia people are limited in the food and other things they can buy. Then when I went to Baltic countries, I saw people who were angry with the Soviet regime . . . It made me think about what my country was.'

Marina met Alexander in 1993 at her thirty-first birthday party. His reputation as an FSB agent preceded him, but (she insists) in a positive way: he had helped out some dance-world friends of hers who were being threatened. 'All his life he believed he served his country . . . I knew his job was dangerous. But he loved his job because he could help people.'

Their son Anatoly was born in June 1994, four months before they married. Life settled down, although Alexander, a workaholic, was always busy and frequently away from home. In November 1998, however, everything changed when he turned whistle-blower, using a TV press conference to expose a KGB plan to kill Boris Berezovsky, the oligarch and former government official. It resulted in Alexander's imprisonment for seven months the following year.

For a while before then Marina had noticed how disillusioned her husband was becoming professionally. 'Sasha became less satisfied with what he was doing. What I heard later was that everything he'd been involved in, he couldn't complete because of all the corruption. It became so high level, linked to high-ranking officers or politicians or businesses. When he told me what they'd been asked to do, I couldn't believe it. They would shoot or kidnap people, it was their duty. Why they decided to give the press conference was that they realised the FSB had become a very dangerous organisation. In 1998, Sasha believed that by talking about this publicly he might change something. This was unfortunately a mistake because it didn't change anything [politically] but it changed our lives absolutely.'

After Alexander's release in 2000, the couple and their young son sought political asylum in the UK with help from Berezovsky. This was granted in May 2001. Once again, things seemed to settle down. But really, it was only a matter of time before Putin got his revenge.

'I couldn't accept that my husband was dying. Nobody believed he was poisoned. I always thought

Sasha would survive . . . I didn't accept he would die because we had just started a normal life here and everything was so good. When he died it's like your world has been completely destroyed. You think you've escaped from these very powerful enemies, but anywhere they will catch you.'

Almost overnight, Marina changed from being a low-key person who didn't want to speak to journalists into the high-profile campaigner she remains today – the result of Sasha, on his deathbed, imploring her to tell their story.

'For two years [afterwards] it was difficult to accept that I am a widow and am famous only because of that. There's a loss of identity there, a real trauma for me when every time I was introduced it was as a widow. And I thought: Am I not capable of more? Can I not do anything else? And this of course gave me the strength to talk and then when we achieved this result and we had the public inquiry [in 2016, chaired by Sir Robert Owen] I felt satisfied because I gave my husband a voice. It gave me strength doing this for him.'

What has happened since Alexander's death is all part of the same love story. Because love, Marina insists, is her motivation. 'To be motivated by hatred is exhausting. But do something for love and you can do it forever.'

Activism is a declaration of hope, a way of life best suited to people with a particular kind of indomitable, sleeves-rolled-up personality. People who have recognised that it is too late to sit back and hope someone else sorts these problems out. And that's the first thing to note: activists have accepted the problem in the first place. And there is something exciting about coming up with solutions, the sheer challenge of recognising that hope cannot be passive.

For too many older people, the future is a redundant abstraction they can't be bothered to invest in. But to the younger generation it's vital and imminent, so much so that they're impatient with waiting to be told what they need to do to bring it about. In his *Letters from Prison*, the philosopher and intellectual Antonio Gramsci talked about how he balanced 'pessimism of the intellect' with 'optimism of the will'. In other words, you can accept that a problem is grave but still find the energy to try to overcome it.

This idea underpins 'Earthrise', a now-famous poem by Amanda Gorman, written in 2018 for the Climate Reality Project, which riffs on the famous titular photograph taken by the *Apollo 8* astronauts of the earth rising over the surface of the moon:

> *There is no rehearsal. The time is*
> *Now*
> *Now*
> *Now,*
> *Because the reversal of harm,*
> *And protection of a future so universal*
> *Should be anything but controversial.*

Which brings me, finally, to Tawakkol Karman, the journalist, politician and human rights activist at the heart of the pro-democracy uprising in her native Yemen.

As a result of her prominent role in the Arab Spring of 2011, Tawakkol became the first Yemeni-Arab woman (and only the second Muslim woman) to be awarded the Nobel Peace Prize for her non-violent struggle for women's rights and gender equality in Yemen and beyond.

Born in 1979, and boasting degrees in both commerce and political science, Tawakkol has long been a vocal critic of the treatment of women in Yemen and has called for their empowerment and inclusion in decision-making processes. To this end, in 2005, she co-founded Women Journalists Without Chains, an organisation which she proudly admits 'made the government so crazy'. When, in 2007, WJWC tried to start its own newspaper and radio station, the Yemeni government, led by the authoritarian President Ali Abdullah Saleh, denied it the necessary permits. Infuriated, Tawakkol and her fellow activists started holding demonstrations in Sana'a's Tahrir Square. 'Journalism and press freedom is a crucial key for democracy,' she says. 'We will not reach democracy without freedom of expression in general and press freedom in particular.'

Tawakkol's arrest on 23 January 2011 triggered an unprecedented wave of protests and catalysed the end of Saleh's three-decade rule, which came a year later after an assassination attempt that left him badly wounded. 'At the time I knew that my voice would become stronger. And that the government was really shaken and I am stronger than them. If they put me in prison or kill me, then the dream that I have fought for and gone to the streets with students for – a dream of freedom and democracy and dignity for my country – absolutely will win.'

All the while Tawakkol wrote articles, gave interviews to global news outlets and tried to ease the transition to a new government, infuriated by Saleh's attempted interference in the process, which only ended with his death in 2017.

The degree to which women led the protests against Saleh was remarkable. As one account puts it: 'Women were encouraged to participate actively in all revolutionary activities and fight side by side with men against the regime and for democratic change . . . They organised marches, led demonstrations, documented events, spread the news through social media and blogs, gave workshops and talks, formed coalitions, made decisions, prepared art programmes, chanted slogans, nursed the wounded, provided food, raised funds, lived and slept outside in tents in the revolutionary squares, just like the men.'[73]

Although she now lives in exile in Istanbul, Tawakkol continues to be an influential and active figure in Yemeni and international politics. The situation in Yemen is currently dire – according to the Council on Foreign Relations, nearly 74 per cent of Yemenis are in need of humanitarian assistance; five million are at risk of famine; and a cholera outbreak has affected over one million people – but Tawakkol remains committed to empowering women and to her belief that 'revolution is a continuous act'.

The brief window in which Yemeni women were permitted to inhabit the public sphere and do what the men were doing closed once patriarchal military and religious leaders infiltrated the protest movements. And as Tawakkol admits, the nature of the struggle has now changed: 'We are now facing the battle against the counter-revolution led by Saudi Arabia, Emirates and Iran . . . Look, when I tell you about my journey, it's not just my journey. It's the journey of every dreamer for freedom and justice and democracy around the world. But [many of them] are dead, and they were doing just what I was doing, so they sacrificed more than me.'

How, I wonder, do you cling on to hope?

'I believe in my dream . . . I believe that all this challenge, all this chaos, is just a temporary chaos. All the winning of the counter-revolution forces is just a fake winning. I believe in people and I know very well the history. All history tells us that every great revolution is followed by a counter-revolution, but at the end the winner will be on the side of the people. In other words, a revolution may seem to fail in the short term, but it will have started a chain of events that may lead to success in the future. I will not lose hope and I advise everyone who is committed to noble values: don't give up and think darkness will prevail.'

WHEN THE WORST HAPPENS . . .

This chapter covers so many different types and levels of adversity that it feels glib to offer one-size-fits-all 'advice'. So I want to focus on the grief and loss that attend serious illness and death and offer up a few observations which, when I was listening to the interview transcripts, struck me as helpful and astute.

- Find a support network — a really good one. Rosamund Adoo-Kissi-Debrah: 'Initially, when a child dies, lots of people are going to be around you. And you know what happens? Life goes back to normal. It's not that they don't care. Life is really, really busy. You have to pick your people. You always need a support network. Try to find people you can call on five years on, eight years on. And they can stop what they're doing for a moment.'

- Be honest with yourself (and other people) about the enormity of what has happened to you. Abi Morgan:

'Don't underestimate that you're in the middle of a thunderstorm – emotionally, physically, practically, economically. I'm not a religious person, but there were literally moments where I'd have to throw my arms up in the air and shout, "Universe, hold me . . ." I had to have something bigger than myself in the hope that I would go forward.'

- Don't be afraid of magical thinking. 'The person you lost will always be with you,' says Marina Litvinenko. 'Maybe in a parallel life, but always with you.' Joan Bakewell, from the vantage point of old age, points out that her attitude to death changed over the years: 'As we lose those dear to us and we sit at bedsides holding their hands, we see that death is a very extraordinary experience, a very important part of life . . . Death gives life its perspective. I have a feeling now that it is quite ordinary and will happen to everybody, including my children and grandchildren, which is unimaginable. In that way I've come to embrace it as part of life, waiting for me at the end. And I want to make the most of every part of my life and enjoy every day.'

6

EMBRACING CHANGE

We've already seen that change is inevitable and constant, though it happens so fast these days it can feel like a peculiarly modern phenomenon. Through the haze of nostalgia the past always feels solid and permanent, even as it recedes at breakneck speed. But change has always been puzzled and angsted over. The Ancient Greek philosopher Heraclitus was known for his doctrine of flux and famously said that no one could step into the same river twice.

As my personal favourite philosopher, Dr Meredith Grey, tells us in *Grey's Anatomy*: 'When we say things like "people don't change" it drives scientists crazy because change is literally the only constant in all of science. Energy. Matter. It's always changing, morphing, merging, growing, dying. It's the way people try not to change that's unnatural. The way we cling to what things were instead of letting things be what they are. The way we cling to old memories instead of forming new ones. The way we insist on believing, despite every scientific indication, that anything in this lifetime is permanent. Change is constant. How we experience change – that's up to us. It can feel like death or it can feel like a second chance at life.'

I couldn't have put it better myself.

At the risk of stating the bleeding obvious, the ability to adapt and evolve leads to new opportunities, growth and success. If it is so obvious, though, why are we not better at it? It's vital, after all. By not embracing change, we may miss out on these opportunities, become stuck in outdated methods or even irrelevant.

Mary Portas's favourite playwright is Arthur Miller. She quoted me a passage from Miller's autobiography, *Timebends*, that had become her personal mantra: 'The desire to move on, to metamorphose – or perhaps it is a talent for being contemporary – was given me as life's inevitable and rightful condition. To keep becoming, always to stay involved in transition.'[74]

'That's been me,' she says. 'And it's a wonderful thing, but it comes with huge pain sometimes because you know that when you do have to move on it affects other people . . .'

At the time we spoke, Portas had recently split from her wife, the journalist Melanie Rickey, and was reeling from the sale of their marital home in north London and the impact of Covid, as well as fearing for the future of her consultancy business, the Portas Agency. Suddenly uncertain about everything, she shed the alpha image for which she had become famous and re-evaluated her whole philosophy.

'I am so over people saying, "What's your passion? Where do you want to be in five years?" It's just the worst thing you can put on any one woman. I've been through this myself and I have a daughter who's now 25. Every time a door opened I just peeked round it and followed so that I could feel where it was taking me . . . I just kept going and knew that ultimately doing my best was going to get me where I needed to go – and I didn't know where I needed to go! So much pressure gets put on people. "You need to know what you want to do." You don't. Just follow stuff that interests you and do your best at it.'

She had moved to Primrose Hill, north London and her three children were with her during lockdown – Verity and Mylo, whose father is her former husband, Graham Portas, and Horatio, who she had with Rickey in 2012, two years before they converted their civil partnership into a same-sex marriage after the law changed.

'I've had an incredible life, but I've had some really, really tough moments. I've just come through one of the worst times, my divorce, and had to sell my house and reestablish my family. During Covid my business dropped by well over half. I turned 60 and I couldn't find joy. There were probably three years of that and only now am I coming out of it.'

The impact of the coronavirus lockdowns on people's professional lives has been well documented. One of the worst-affected sectors, alongside retail and hospitality, was entertainment. Classical musicians suffered greatly as live performances, which make up a significant portion of their income, were cancelled or postponed. The closure of concert halls and music venues led to a sharp decline in their work opportunities, leaving many musicians without a source of income. Additionally, the pandemic resulted in the postponement or cancellation of festivals, tours and other events, causing financial strain for musicians who rely on these events to make a living.

Jess Gillam is a British saxophonist and classical musician. Born in 1998, she rose to prominence after reaching the final of the BBC Young Musician of the Year competition in 2016. Since then she has established herself as one of the leading saxophonists in the UK and performed with numerous orchestras and ensembles, including the BBC Philharmonic, the Royal Northern Sinfonia and the London Sinfonietta.

Frustrated by lockdown but determined to do something to ease the plight of her fellow musicians, she founded the Virtual Scratch Orchestra (VSO), a project designed to encourage children and young people to get involved in music-making and programming by giving them the opportunity to participate in a virtual orchestra. Musicians were able to contribute by arranging and composing music using the visual programming language Scratch and uploading their recordings so that they could be combined with others to form a full orchestral performance.

'I felt so sorry not just for younger players but all musicians,' Gillam tells me. 'The best thing about being able to play with other people in a band or orchestra is being part of something bigger than yourself – the community that music can offer.'

Gillam expected perhaps 50 people to take part in the VSO. 'But across the three projects we had over 2,000 musicians from right across the world. It was one of the most uplifting experiences, just to see how much people crave that togetherness. It took a long time [to put together], but it was worth it.'

The VSO is a brilliant example of change being embraced because it shows how easy it can be to adapt when you have to. Confronted by lockdown, Gillam thought laterally and turned to new technologies to find a solution. Using video conferencing and music production software to collaborate overcame the limitations – as we then had to think of them – of playing music together, live and in person.

At her Catholic convent school Anya Hindmarch, founder of the eponymous luxury goods brand, developed a passion for choral singing – 'vespers, vigils, candlelit mass, all those things' – and for a time it was something she considered doing professionally. But then disaster struck. 'I had one really bad performance in a school music production which threw me for years. I missed my introduction and my lovely music teacher said, "Don't worry, we'll try it again." I tried it again and missed the introduction again! It was just nerves, but I remember I really wanted the floor to swallow me up, for me not to be there.

'It took me years to get over it. Afterwards, I always had a fear of public speaking and standing in front of people. I decided that that was ridiculous so I explored something called neurolinguistic programming, which essentially removes the trauma of the bad experience, in my case the singing competition, and scrubs it from your brain by different exercises. It worked in one session and my fear suddenly became manageable.'

Meanwhile, at the other end of the spectrum, it was

fear of *not* performing that led actress Juliet Stevenson to give up a place at Bristol University and go to RADA instead. 'I left school, had a place, then had another lightbulb moment,' she explained to me. 'I woke up and thought: What am I doing? Why am I going to read this as an academic subject when that's not my relationship to it? I want to act. I want to be people, other people, tell other people's stories in my body. I don't want to study plays academically. So I wrote to RADA, which was the only place I'd heard of, and said how do you get in and they said you do an audition. So I prepared two pieces pretty much on my own. I walked in, did it, then they read out a list of people which I thought was a list of the people they wanted to leave – because they shortlist you on the same day and if you get shortlisted then you audition again in the afternoon. So I put on my coat and walked out of the building. The doorman, John, came after me and said, "Where do you think you're going? You're on the shortlist . . ." When the letter arrived telling me I'd got a place, I could not believe it. In that second everything became clear, really. My world went from blurred to sharp focus.'

Her debut Royal Shakespeare Company stage performance was similarly unexpected and a baptism of fire. But Stevenson knew she had no choice but to embrace uncertainty and do as she was told. 'It was 1978, the RSC called and said, "Can you be on a train at 2 p.m. today?" A girl in the cast of *The Tempest*, a star-studded production with Alan Rickman, Michael Hordern and David Suchet, had broken her leg. She'd been playing a Sea Nymph and a Hellhound. I was pulled off the train, driven into Stratford. They took my coat and case off me and pushed me straight into the wings where the last dress rehearsal was going on.

'There was a little person in front of me and they said, "Look, just do whatever she does on stage, talk to you later . . ." So when this little person ran onto the stage and barked, I ran onto the stage and barked. She flapped her arms around and so did I. It turned out to be Ruby Wax. She was Hellhound and Sea Nymph number one and I was number two.'

Sometimes following an unpredictable path can be satisfying, particularly if you're someone who has often felt out of sync with your peers. It lends purpose to feelings of isolation and apartness that might otherwise be disabling. After she finished school, Kirstie Allsopp decided not to go to university. 'I hadn't enjoyed school and university just seemed to me to be another group of kids of my age, except now they were drinking more beer and taking drugs, which frightened me and I didn't see the point. I just thought: I'll get out into the grown-up environment of work – and I was right. I enjoyed it much more.'

Kirstie worked for a short while in interior design and then in magazine journalism and thought that would be her career. Her move into TV was unplanned and unsought and came about after she had left *Country Living* magazine and was doing a History of Art course, having felt that she had 'missed out on some educational elements' by skipping university. 'While I was doing that, a friend asked another friend to find a flat that was similar to the one my friend had, and that's how we started out finding flats for people.' One of her fledgling company's clients was the *Guardian* journalist Jonathan Freedland, who was so impressed by their work that he wrote an article ('without telling me or my then business partner, Miranda') and put their phone number at the bottom.

After that, things went berserk. The calls didn't stop. One of them was from a TV production company. 'We said no, absolutely not. A fly-on-the-wall documentary about two Sloaney girls is the last thing we want. Then six months later another company called and we said yes [to a meeting] out of sheer greed because they took us to the River Cafe. And they did a screen test and made a non-transmittable pilot – thank God no one will ever see it – with me and the great, wonderful Phil Spencer and that's how we met. We stayed at a hotel in Lewes and he thought I was bonkers because I came down to have a drink with no shoes on and he said, "You can't not wear shoes!"'

It's one thing making or submitting to a change yourself. That's almost always positive and empowering, even if the result is disappointing in the end, because you chose to do it. It's much more difficult to accept a change in your life when it's imposed upon you externally. Yet this does happen to an awful lot of people.

The biggest changes affecting the world today are the result of wars and the climate emergency. One of the ways human populations adapt to environmental changes is migration. And all the evidence suggests that, as a result of this, immigrant populations are exceptionally resourceful and good at coping with change and adversity. It's why, as Ian Goldin, Professor of Globalisation and Development at the University of Oxford, has written, 'governments that are more open to immigration assist their country's businesses, which become more agile, adaptive and profitable in the war for talent.'[75]

On average, immigrants contribute twice as much to US entrepreneurship as native-born citizens do. But immigrants aren't just creating more businesses: they're creating more successful ones. A 2018 Harvard Business School study by William Kerr and Sari Pekkala Kerr concluded that immigrant-led companies grew faster and were more likely to survive in the long term than their native-led rivals.

William Kerr thinks this is because 'the very act of someone moving around the world, often leaving family behind, might select those who are very determined or more tolerant of business risk'.[76] He points out that migrating to a new country requires a high level of tolerance for uncertainty.

That will be passed down to children too. So the need to change is hardwired in. Ironically but understandably, this adaptability is sometimes channelled into ensuring a no-nonsense stability that for future generations can come to seem like a straitjacket.

I sensed this when I spoke to the entrepreneur Nisha Katona, founder of the restaurant chain Mowgli Street Food. A former child protection barrister, she grew up with doctor parents who had very set expectations when it came to their daughter's career choices.

'Generally in the immigrant Asian population there is a pressure not just for you to be a doctor, but for you to be financially useful to the nation that you come to; for you to have a job that they can't sack you from easily. It was very much born from insecurity. Our work ethic is: if you do not work harder and if you are not more useful than the next person, then you will fall off the face of Britain. And I was born in this country! I am basically a brown-white person; I'm basically an English person with more melanin.

'Yet I was raised with this real insecurity, partly because of what we suffered in the early days. I was born in 1971 in a very working-class town in the north-west [Ormskirk in Lancashire] that is my home and I love it. The reason that happened is that in those days, when Enoch Powell was beckoning across doctors from the East, we could only work in towns that no white doctor would go to. So very often you were in these working-class northern towns where there was real deprivation. So that's the crucible in which all my emotions were formed, my earliest memories were of firebombs in the garden and a brick coming through my nursery window with the word "P" written on it. And that was par for the course. My mother would be stoned on the way to the surgery by the very people she would be treating.'

Nisha started off studying Psychology. 'By then I had pretty much come off the rails and my family had given up. You're raised to go out with the person you're going to marry after you meet them at medical school. There's so much presumption in all of that because a) I wasn't clever enough to go to medical school, and b) at 17 I started going out with a boy I wasn't allowed to see.'

One day, however, while she was doing part-time filing work at a firm of solicitors, she was sent to court to deliver a brief to a barrister. 'I remember walking into those chambers and the scales falling from my eyes. I thought: My God, there is such a job as this . . .' She switched from Psychology to Law, later defying expectations by becoming the first female Indian barrister in Liverpool.

'What I'm proudest of is that my circuitous route came from failure. I failed my A-levels, failed to get into medical school, failed to engage with and love Psychology. All these doors close for a reason.'

As it happened, other doors were about to open for Nisha. Food had always been one of her great loves and she had taught Indian cooking on the side while working as a barrister. It was at this point that she had the idea for Mowgli. 'I was passionate about the way Indians ate at home. Once you get that idea in your head, that sense that you have an idea for something that represents a complete gap in the market, you just think: why am I not doing it? At first I didn't want to do it because the media made it look like you had to be a psychopathic beast to run a kitchen.' So she changed the script. 'When I did finally build Mowgli it was with a zero tolerance policy [for that kind of behaviour]. And now we're building our twenty-first restaurant.'

It was a similar story for another chef, Romy Gill, who started cooking in earnest as a child when her mother became ill. 'When she had cancer I was in the sixth form and that's when I got into it, when I understood it and took on more of it, because it was always very much her job. My dad also enjoyed cooking. He found it therapeutic. I started with my dad, grinding the spices, pickling or just making curry. Then I went on and started learning with Mum. But when I told my dad I wanted to go into hospitality he said, "No way, you won't survive."'

Aged just 22, Romy followed her husband to the UK. The excitement of being in a new place lasted all of a week, then she became 'so depressed'. She had no friends and at that time, the early 1990s, phoning home to speak to her family in India cost a fortune. 'I missed home, especially the food. My husband said, "Let's go to an Indian restaurant" and so we did. But it was so sweet and everything tasted the same, of the same generic sauce. I said, "I'm going to open an Indian restaurant" – and my husband looked at me as if to say, this woman is going to do it.

'I started catering, inviting people to dinner parties, making samosas the way I'd learned from grandmother. She always made me look closely at how she was making them. I kept on doing it when I moved to the Southwest, then went on to teaching schools, food fairs, standing in cold wet weather! I felt a sense of belonging, like: "This is what I want to do, this is where I belong, whether it is hot or cold."'

Sure enough, Romy became the first female Indian chef to open a restaurant in the UK – and with a daughter who was just six months old at the time. Getting it off the ground was far from easy. Having sold jewellery and shares, Romy then tried to get a bank loan, only to be refused. 'The BBC came to know that we were trying to get a loan and we were featured on the national news.' The next day, NatWest agreed to provide the loan and Romy's Kitchen opened in Thornbury, outside Bristol, in 2013, closing six years later after her lease on the building expired. The closure saddened Romy but enabled her to focus more on her media and writing work. In 2016, she was awarded an MBE for Services to Hospitality.

'I was the chef and the owner and I'd never thought of being the first anything,' she explained. 'But getting that recognition was very important to me as a self-taught woman coming from a small town in India.'

Another form of imposed, external change is illness or an accident. As it happens, I tripped and fell in the street the other day, landing on my knees and spraining a ligament. So I am writing this with my left leg elevated as per the instructions of the nice nurse at Guy's Hospital who dressed my wounds and packed me off for an X-ray. In the scheme of things they were very minor injuries, but any accident makes you think 'what if?', rather as a near-miss car smash can leave you almost as unsettled as the real thing.

I love the phrase that became the title for the English-language edition of the photographer Henri Cartier-Bresson's famous book: 'the decisive moment'. 'To me,' he wrote, 'photography is the simultaneous recognition, in a fraction of a second, of the significance of an event.' Such 'photographic' moments are scattered throughout our lives. They can be either positive or negative, but they always contain an element of shock, an electrical discharge like the popping of an old-style flash bulb.

'Life changes fast. Life changes in the instant. You sit down to dinner and life as you know it ends.'[77] These were the first words Joan Didion wrote after her husband, John Gregory Dunne, died mid-conversation of a massive heart attack as Joan was about to serve up dinner. 'My attention was on mixing the salad. John was talking, then he wasn't.'[78]

She called the Microsoft Word file 'notes on change. doc' and the book that file eventually became, the extraordinary *The Year of Magical Thinking*, is really a meditation on change which builds to the horrifying realisation that to a grieving widow change means decay; that 'as the days pass . . . certain things will happen. My image of John at the instant of his death will become less immediate, less raw . . . My sense of John himself, John alive, will become more remote, even "mudgy", softened, transmuted into whatever best serves my life without him.'[79]

The most shocking thing about the accident that befell the dotcom entrepreneur Martha Lane Fox, apart from the brutality of it, is how young she was when it happened: just 31.

When, with her business partner Brent Hoberman, Martha founded the travel and leisure company last-minute.com, she was riding the crest of the noughties dotcom boom. She stepped down as managing director at the end of 2003 and in 2005 the company was sold in a deal that valued it at £577 million.

Martha emerged from the sale a very wealthy woman. But her ability to enjoy her newfound riches was compromised by the fact that she was, at the time, in hospital recovering from the 'catastrophic' car crash she had been involved in the previous year while on holiday in Morocco. It left her with 28 broken bones and nearly killed her.

As she told me: 'I was so unable to really think about anything except if I was going to be able to walk again, if I was going to be able to get out of hospital.'

I wondered what, if anything, she remembered about the day of the crash?

'Nothing at all. I remember something about the day before and I have patches of memory of being in Morocco, of moving hospitals in Morocco, but nothing for the first few weeks. I spent two years in hospital in all. I was allowed to go home after about a year, for a month, then I had to go back for six or nine months, I can't remember – there were more surgeries and more physio and recovery. It was pretty hideous but the flipside is I had incredible support, amazing doctors, carers and nurses.

'On one level I coped because every single day for that whole period someone came to see me, my friends wrote me letters . . . They were astonishing and continued to be so careful and caring over such a long period of time. I remember them showing movies on the ceiling of my hospital room and bringing their newborn babies and putting them beside me. The other thing is that I am a stubborn and determined person, so give me some targets that feel real to me and that's very motivating. Even if the target was that I could lift my arm to 10 degrees from zero, or be able to stand for one and a half seconds, that was how I measured out my life.'

You never fully recover from an accident like Martha's. Even now, she gets tired easily and is in constant pain. She was desperate to continue working, but recognised that in order to work at all she would have to do things completely differently. The result has been a spectacular 'portfolio' career. Among other things, she created the Government Digital Service to improve access to online public services; co-founded the Lucky Voice karaoke bar chain; sat on the board of Twitter/X (until recently); and founded the thinktank Doteveryone.

'I was thrown into this portfolio life really young,' she said. 'I was 37, 38, by the time I'd come through the accident enough to function. I can't do one big job anymore because I'm just too physically choppy and I have to have time out. So I've built up this portfolio life which is fantastic in many ways because I can be across the public sector, the private sector, work in the House of Lords [she is a cross-bench peer, Baroness Lane Fox of Soho], see all these interesting organisations and not have to be in a team or an office. It feels a luxury to pull threads across companies as seemingly far apart as Chanel and Twitter/X, but they are similar challenges in some dimensions.'

The other change she had to deal with was becoming disabled, with all the discrimination and sidelining that still comes with that. 'I feel as if I became more invisible after the accident, though you're more visible in some ways when you have two sticks as I do. Certainly, there's a layer of life that goes. It's hard to explain. People see your sticks rather than you walking down the street. Then you add ageing into it too . . .'

For this reason, Martha has taken to having a pink streak in her hair and always wears bright clothes. 'It's to say, "Hello! I'm still here!"' she laughs.

I said earlier that a ladder is a scaffold for climbing through thin air. That's certainly what it must have felt like for the head of Meta's Global Business Group, Nicola Mendelsohn, on the day she was diagnosed with follicular lymphoma, an incurable cancer of the blood.

'The first thing that went through my mind was: Am I going to die?' she admitted. 'That's what you think when you hear the word cancer. You don't get told that word straight away. My experience was that they were teasing me to that point because it's such a lot of information to take in in one go. From there it was just the greatest jumble of negative thoughts: not being able to see my children grow up, not seeing grandchildren, all the dreams . . . It was really awful. I was diagnosed on a Friday and it was without doubt the worst weekend of my life.'

Well, almost diagnosed. 'We had to wait till Monday to talk to experts as we weren't sure what kind of cancer it was. I spent the weekend crying, not sleeping, Googling what it might be, what the consequences would be, what the life expectancy might be. We thought it was best not to tell the children until we had more information because why worry people more? Also, the range of things it could have been was pretty vast, so that first weekend was just John and I having a pretty horrible time.'

When the time did come to tell the children, 'I couldn't get the words out. They knew it was serious, they could see our behaviour was different. I just remember their faces looking so little and worried. Zac, our youngest, was 11 at the time and I remember him asking, "Are you going to die?" I said, "I hope not. I'm going to give it my best shot but I can't make you promises I can't keep."

'In terms of cancer this is incurable, but you can live with it. You need multiple treatments and your body will become ravaged by the impact of the treatment fighting off the cancer, but you can live with it and live a full life.'

At the time we spoke, Mendelsohn was in remission. I asked her if, even so, she was constantly checking herself for symptoms?

'Yes, but I also think back to how I felt that first weekend. I had a conscious conversation with myself that I didn't want to let it define my life. What I also realised was that if I allow myself to be dictated by negative thoughts and thinking it will destroy me. I mean, I literally lost half a stone in weight that weekend from worrying – the physical angst and the crying. And I thought: I'm not going to ravage myself like this. I'm going to get myself as strong as I can, I'm going to learn as much as I can about this disease and I'm going to do my best.'

Did she consider giving up work?

'Lots of people asked me that at the start and I thought: No, I love my job, I love what I do. It's such a massive part of me and if I didn't have that I'd literally just be sat at home worrying about cancer every day. Given that I am well and am fit, there's no reason not to [work].'

The illness changed her in all sorts of ways. She admits that before it she 'hadn't really done a lot of soul-searching in my life'. Post-diagnosis, she thought 'about how I use my time, the values I hold dear, the friends and family. In that respect I was lucky as some people come out of a diagnosis and they change jobs, change partners. For me there was nothing dramatic like that. It just gave me a greater sense of gratitude.

'I do an exercise on vision writing and I do it every year. You write your vision as though it's a year from now, thinking through what I want to achieve across three buckets: my family, my work and my community. It goes back to the Jewish concept of *tikkun olam* (healing the world), which is that people who give back to their community are happier.'

Screenwriter and playwright Abi Morgan has written a wonderful book, *This Is Not A Pity Memoir*, about her dual experience of sudden, life-changing illness. First, it was that of her then partner (now husband), actor Jacob Krichefski. Jacob, who has MS, complained one morning about feeling unwell. Abi, in a rush to get the kids to school so that she could start work, told him snappily to take a paracetamol before exiting the house. When she arrived home later, he was lying comatose on the bathroom floor. Later she learns that he has suffered a hideous reaction to being taken off a supposed wonder drug for his MS.

Jacob was put into an induced coma – for seven months. When finally he woke, he was not just physically debilitated but a changed person who had no idea who Abi was; who believed, in fact, that the woman sitting in front of him was an impostor pretending to be the mother of his children. 'Something was severed, the emotional connection with who I was.'

As if that wasn't enough, while Jacob was in hospital Abi was diagnosed with a rare, aggressive form of breast cancer. Add to this a mass of pandemic-related complications and you have pretty much the biggest nightmare imaginable.

Except that Abi coped. Her life – and her partner's, and her children's – had been turned upside down. But her instinct, long honed, was to try to see it all through her screenwriter's eyes. By May 2019, when her cancer diagnosis came through, 'I was mainly really irritated, because in the book of the film of the life of this experience, it felt like a really naff plot point. I thought: I just can't put this in a movie, it's unbelievable. It deserves a movie of its own. Though I'm not sure I would want to watch that film.'

Related to embracing change is being attentive to what we might call the music of chance. This means accepting that there isn't a plan and that stuff happens in life for the weirdest reasons.

It's natural to want assurances that if we behave in a certain way, the future will unfold in a certain way. But as the late, great Susan Jeffers, author of the self-help bestseller *Feel The Fear And Do It Anyway*, pointed out in another of her books, *Embracing Uncertainty*, we can't control the world in that way. What's more, if we could then we wouldn't want to use that control as much as we think. 'Strangely, as much as we worry about the uncertainty of the future, I believe that if someone could tell us in advance how things were going to turn out, we wouldn't like to hear it.'[80] Knowing would spoil things, Jeffers writes, like someone revealing the plot of a film we haven't seen. If we can 'transfer the feelings of upset, even panic, about the future' into the understanding that we can benefit from this uncertainty then that's progress.

It's helpful in this context to consider a story Eileen Atkins told me about how she became first a dancer and then an actress: that it only happened at all because her mother was scared of gypsies. 'She knocked on our door and she looked so exotic, very different, with her earrings and the scarf around her head. She looked straight at me and pointed at me with a bony finger and said, "That little one there is going to be a great dancer, another Pavlova." And that was it, my mother went to find a dancing class immediately. She didn't get me into one until I was five because I kept screaming and saying "take me home, I don't want to dance" – but finally she got me into a place called the KY School. And there was a very weird dancing teacher who called herself Madame Kavos Yandie when her name was really Kathleen Smith. She came from Peckham but she told us she was Spanish . . . She took a particular interest in me, though I don't think I was particularly good, and turned me into Baby Eileen who tap-danced in working men's clubs for 15 bob a go and sang the most unsuitable songs.'

Mary Portas thought she knew exactly what she was going to do with her life: go to RADA and become an actress. But then, when she was 16, her mother died of meningitis. Her father, who was in his early fifties, 'just collapsed', leaving Mary to look after her younger brother. Eighteen months later her father moved in with his new wife. When, two years later, he too died suddenly, her stepmother (to whom he'd left everything) threw Mary out of the family house and sold it.

'You had to survive and cope. So you didn't make choices based on [what] the right one [was], you made it on survival. How do I keep this job? Make sure I'm financially okay?'

Adjoa Andoh wouldn't have become an actress – and certainly not *Bridgerton*'s Lady Danbury – if she'd stuck with her original career: Lloyds Bank's loss was our gain. She told the story of her twisty route to stage and screen with a breeziness that made me laugh.

'I was terrible [in the bank], rubbish with numbers. I was the person whose bank balances didn't balance at the end of the day. I'd wanted to read Law at Cambridge but in the sixth form everything collapsed, so I didn't. Then I redid my A-levels. Then I decided I'd done with education, I was going to work in a bank, move in with my boyfriend, potter about in the Cotswolds and be happy. But after a year at the bank I was running back towards education going, "Yes! I will do that Law degree!" So I moved to Bristol and went to Bristol Polytechnic, which had a fantastic Law department. Did a year and a half. Absolutely hated it.

'Really, I wanted to be an actor, but where I grew up no one was an actor. I might as well have wanted to be an astronaut. While I was doing my degree I'd joined a black women's group. We went to Greenham Common, things like that, and my whole world expanded in terms of literature and performance and storytelling. When I packed in my Law degree – it made my dad weep – a woman from my group who taught drama, Deb'bora Imani, got some money to put on a show in London and asked me to be involved. I thought I'd be there for two weeks, but I never went back.'

Sometimes the trick is to perceive change that's happening elsewhere – in a particular institution, say, or elsewhere in the culture – and put yourself in a position where you can embrace or even benefit from that change. When Frances Morris, now Director of Tate Modern, first joined the Tate in 1987 she found it 'very old-fashioned, with very few exhibitions – a real retreat from the world'. But as it transpired that point marked 'the beginning of real change and I feel incredibly lucky that I joined at a point where everything was up for discussion, up for grabs'.

'We were able to take on the newly launched Turner Prize,' she explained, 'and be instrumental in setting up a new commissioning space, the Art Now room, which is still going strong.' With Mrs Thatcher in Number 10, museums and other cultural institutions were having to adjust to new realities. As Morris puts it: 'They had to take more responsibility for themselves. Therefore they became more entrepreneurial, which was both a good and a bad thing. There was a precarity and fragility associated with having to generate our own income, but it did mean that in the 1980s we had to command our own destinies. So there was a lot of thinking about the future: strategies and visions. It wasn't like business-as-usual and I found that incredibly exciting.'

When, at the height of the Covid pandemic in the UK, the venture capitalist Kate Bingham was first asked to lead the government's vaccine task force, her instinct was to refuse, both because she had little confidence that effective vaccines could be found and for a more mundane reason. 'My first reaction was that I wasn't a vaccine expert,' she said. 'I got a ticking-off from my daughter who said that I was doing myself down and I should get on and do it. In hindsight, the skills that I brought were the right sort of skills.'

This is important, I think. When you make a change in your life, especially your professional life, you're not throwing away everything you did up to that point. And when change happens to women, they are often better placed to cope with it than they think because they inevitably have more experience than they give themselves credit for.

Kate didn't know anything about vaccines, but she knew about risk, backing the mRNA vaccines when the technology had never been successfully used before. Her outsider status was useful and gave her the armour to cope with the flack and what she describes as 'distraction, in my case quite politically driven', which often came from within Downing Street itself.

Change is about keeping things fresh. When we're tired we talk about wanting a 'change of scene'. Some people go further and have a 'change of life'.

Between 1962 and 1969, while she was married to the director Michael Bakewell, Joan Bakewell had an affair with the playwright Harold Pinter. Since revealing this fact to the world in the 1990s – to Michael Billington, who was writing a biography of Pinter –

Joan has consistently defended the affair rather than go down the expected route (for a woman) of saying she feels guilty and regrets it. Her reason for doing this, she told me, is because the affair represented a conscious moral act, a deliberate decision to live differently.

'I remember making the decision to face an option in life that was dangerous and perhaps wrong in most people's eyes and possibly my own. But I thought: You can either say yes to this or say no and think about it. And it was such a compelling relationship that I thought: This may be wrong. It may be disapproved of. But I'm going to say yes to this and go ahead.

'And so it was a very conscious decision in that it flew in the face of certainly the morality I'd grown up with and the morality I tried to live by. I deliberately defied my own values because I could not resist the compulsion of that bond.'

Being open and flexible involves admitting not that you're wrong necessarily – because if it's a matter of opinion who's to say whether you are or not? – but that there's another side to an issue you perhaps hadn't considered fully. When she was Education Secretary (and holder of the equalities brief), Nicky Morgan voted against gay marriage, saying she believed marriage was between 'a man and a woman'. In 2014, she changed her mind and announced that she would vote for it if given the chance again.

'Both in life and in politics we expect people not to change their minds,' she said to me, 'and I'm not quite sure why. Because actually I think you're a better politician, and probably a better person in life generally, if you have looked at something and been made to think again and realise that actually there is a better way of tackling a problem, another point of view. And yet we seem to say to people, "That's it, we should never talk to you again because you changed your view." I don't think that's how life works.'

We hear a lot today about how dogmatic and prone to cancelling people Generation Z supposedly is. So I was pleasantly surprised when I interviewed the 20-year-old conservationist and environmental activist Bella Lack for *The Ladder*. Bella is an astonishing force of nature. In her late teens she combined studying for her A-levels with writing a book, *The Children of the Anthropocene*, for which she spoke to young people like herself from across the world, each of them engaged in a project to address the climate emergency: for example, the two Indonesian sisters who went on a hunger strike to try to persuade the governor of Bali to ban plastic bags from the island. As well as making a documentary with the primatologist Jane Goodall – *Animal*, selected for the 2021 Cannes Film Festival – she is an ambassador for the Born Free Foundation.

Bella's interest in the environment began when she was around 11 or 12. 'Before then I'd been the kind of child who would go into the garden and bring in snails and leave them in Tupperware containers around the kitchen. Then I watched a documentary about palm oil. I remember it was quite a viral video at the time. It showed a mother orangutan with her child in a palm oil monoculture and it's almost impossible for species to survive in this monoculture because there's so little biodiversity.'

The depredations wreaked by the palm oil industry

on natural habitats became an early focus for Bella's activism. But then she started to wonder if she'd got her facts absolutely right; or rather, whether there might be other targets more deserving of her anger and energy.

'At the beginning I was so wrong about the palm oil thing,' she says now. 'I'd say that we needed to boycott palm oil and it turns out that isn't a solution because it's more sustainable than other types of oil we use.'

It's impressive, especially for an activist committed to promoting a particular viewpoint, to admit when she's changed her mind or discovered that an approach has been wrong or misguided.

'Yes,' she agrees, 'especially an activist of my age because there's still so much I don't know. I've changed how I do activism so much. When I started working with the Born Free Foundation, lots of people know [actress] Virginia McKenna and the story of the lions. We as humans relate a lot to individuals [like McKenna]. It's called psychic numbing: we can't relate to masses. Before that, I was churning out statistics saying things like "we have twelve years left to prevent catastrophic climate change and by 2050 there'll be more plastic in oceans than fish". But actually we relate better to individual stories. You see that with Cecil the lion [who was killed by big-game trophy hunters] and Harambe the gorilla [who was shot by a zoo worker when a child climbed into his enclosure]. Those stories catalyse this massive engagement.

'It's all about flexibility. Pursuing a goal, but being

flexible. When I felt I wasn't being effective, I changed from railing against the system to looking to what we want in 2050. A lot more of what I do now is about hope for the future. Our generation actually has a chance to change society. It's better to be hopeful, to trade in solutions, rather than telling people what's wrong – because there's *so much* wrong.'

Depending on who you ask, AI is either one of those wrong things, a blot on the landscape of our human future, or a universal panacea that will cure cancer, find new galaxies and mitigate the climate emergency in the time it takes us to pour oat milk on our bran flakes.

Before AI gets to work, however, it needs to sort itself out, gender-wise, lest it undoes the years of work women have put into fighting gender inequality. AI is developed by humans, therefore it mirrors human behaviour and internalises all the biases we already have, as well as adding a few of its own just for fun. An example of this is the notorious Amazon 'assisted hiring' incident of a few years back, where the tech company's use of AI to make its recruitment processes fairer and more efficient blew up in its face after the AI decided for itself that it was better not to hire women.[81]

Gender bias is introduced during machine learning. If not enough women contribute to building the dataset used by the AI then there will be holes in its knowledge. ('Can you imagine if all the toddlers in the world were raised by 20-year-old men?' asked Frida Polli, CEO of Pymetrics, a company that tries to improve the efficiency and diversity of hiring. 'That's what our

AI looks like today. It's being built by a very homogenous group.'[82])

One British woman who is doing her best to fight this is the self-described 'tech evangelist' Sue Black, who leads the #BiasinAI UK Network from her office at Durham University where she is a Professor of Computer Science.

Sue is remarkable not just for her intellectual acuity – or her shock of spiky red hair, or her readiness to state baldly that society is misogynist – but for how hard she had to work to get where she is. Hers is a survivor's story, but also a lesson in ladder-climbing: namely, that the second half of your life can be radically different from the first half if you choose to make it so.

Her normal, comfortable childhood was disrupted when Sue's mother died when she was 12. 'At around 11 o'clock one morning my mother said she had a headache and went to bed . . . I said to my dad – both of my parents were nurses and I used to read a lot of medical textbooks – "I think Mum's had a brain haemorrhage", just on the basis of the symptoms she was displaying. And that was in fact what had happened.' She was just 34.

After her father remarried, to a woman who made Sue and her two siblings' lives difficult, she left home and school (at 16, before taking her A-levels) and at 18 fell into an abusive relationship with the man who would become her first husband. 'He had quite a volatile temper. I remember one time he tried to strangle me on the washing machine, which seems quite comic, thinking back, but awful at the same time obviously. He threw things at the wall and shouted and broke stuff.'

I'm struck, I tell Sue, by how matter-of-fact she is when describing his behaviour.

'It's probably time. It's a long time ago now, 1987, and it feels like another life. It doesn't bear any resemblance to my life for the past twenty-five years so I feel very distant from it.'

Sue ran away from him 'with three small children and a suitcase, first thing in the morning' and sought shelter in a women's refuge. There she climbed the first rung of the ladder whose top she would reach nearly forty years later, studying A-level Maths at Southwark College, then a degree in Computing and a PhD in Software Engineering. All of this with three small children and very limited money and childcare. On subsequently becoming a lecturer at South Bank University, the first thing Sue did with her pay cheque was buy some clothes. 'I remember going to the big Marks & Spencer on Oxford Street and asking the woman at the till if it was all right to get dressed in the new clothes I'd just bought. She said yes, so I went into the changing room and put them on, then put my old clothes in a carrier bag and ceremoniously dumped them in the bin outside because they were full of holes. I'm getting goosebumps now, just remembering being able to do that.'

Sue recognised what's become known as the 'digital divide' between men and women very early on. In 1998, after attending conferences where she was usually one of the only women present, she set up BCSWomen, the UK's first online network for women in tech. After this came a successful high-profile campaign to save Bletchley Park and #techmums, a social enterprise designed for mothers who felt left behind by what their kids were up to online.

She feels passionately about opening up the tech world to women and making it a comfortable place. 'When I set up BCSWomen I thought I was setting up this really cool network and one male colleague said, "Why are you ghettoising yourself?" I just thought: What? Where's that coming from? The percentage of women in tech back then was 15 or 20 per cent and now it's about the same, which is terrible. But the attitude has changed.'

Now 61, Sue herself has changed beyond all recognition from the cowed, powerless figure she once was. I love the image of her confidently shaking the then Prince Charles's hand when in 2016 she received her OBE for Services to Technology. 'I found a massive difference later in life,' she says. 'Now, I've got a massively supportive, lovely husband, and having just one person who really supports you can make a major, major difference.'

Perhaps this is why Sue is so fired up by the desire to change others, to ensure that the march of digital progress doesn't leave anyone behind. We are surrounded by technology now – in our cars, fridges and central heating systems – and no one, least of all women, can afford to be a Luddite. 'The more you understand about that technology and how it works, it gives you power over your life – and over your future.'

HOW TO EMBRACE CHANGE

- Don't try to escape change by pretending it hasn't happened. Instead, deal with it proactively – even anticipate it, e.g. by booking a doctor's appointment before you really need to.

- Routines are vital. Try to keep mealtimes and bedtimes regular. Walking the dog, exercising, winding down – try to do them at the same time every day.

- Stay off social media. At times of crisis it's natural to want to vent and/or seek out allies. But places like Instagram are no good when you're feeling vulnerable. Comparing your 'changed-for-the-worse' life to that of someone whose good fortune seems (though probably isn't) constant will only make you feel worse.

- Professor Sue Black: 'Find people around you who will support you who are going through the same thing as you.'

- Remember that change is an inevitable part of life and its outcomes are as likely to be positive as negative. Chances are, you have already successfully navigated your way through a whole landslide of changes in your life without realising that was what you were doing. Recall the skills and strengths you used then – and apply them now.

AFTERWORD

Throughout these pages, aided by a glorious regiment of contributors to my Times Radio show, I've tried to explore some of the main challenges faced by women as they climb the ladder of life, from imposter syndrome to workplace harassment. The testimonies gathered here show the profound effects these hurdles have on women's personal and professional lives, limiting their opportunities and stunting their growth. But I hope they also show how effectively women have fought back.

For some valedictory words of wisdom, who better to turn to than Professor Dame Mary Beard, probably Britain's most famous Classicist? She recently retired from teaching at Cambridge University after forty years. 'I think you have to know when you're ready to go, when you're ready to change,' she muses when we speak. 'Cambridge happens to have a fixed retirement age, but I was very happy with that.' She left with a splash, making a 'retirement gift' which will help to fund two Classics students from under-represented backgrounds as part of efforts to encourage more diversity among those studying the subject.

Dame Mary's pre-eminence in her field is such that it seems always to have existed as a fact. So it's gratifying to learn that she excelled even as an undergraduate; though depressing that, even then – many years before the late journalist AA Gill wrote that she should be 'kept away from cameras' because she was 'too ugly for television' – men were belittling her achievements.

'Being brought up in a single-sex school, I didn't realise – and this was colossally naive – that sexism would affect me because it never had . . . Now, in some ways when I got to university (even though I was at a single-sex college, but it was a mixed university) I did find that [it affected me], not so much among the staff but among the other students . . . I remember a guy who's still a friend picking up an essay of mine from the floor of my very messy room. My tutor had written on the bottom, "This is very good, it would get a First" and the guy said, "What, *you*? Get a First?" And I thought, you're only saying that because I'm a woman. If we were in a man's room, you wouldn't say that. So I think that gave me iron in my soul to think not that I felt *personally* outraged by this – *politically* I was, but not personally – but that this was very silly and wrong. A lot of sexism is just silly. If you think of it as that, it's a lot easier to deal with. Of course,' she qualifies, 'some of it is not silly, but some of it is.'

The double standards that persist in how women are judged – on their appearance, behaviour and career choices – can lead to a constant fear of falling short. The pressure to be a perfect mother, partner and professional can be overwhelming. Too many women feel they must be flawless in every aspect of their lives and when inevitably they fall short of these ideals it reinforces a belief that they are not good enough.

This perpetuates a cycle of inequality. When women do not believe in their abilities and potential, they are less likely to negotiate for equal pay, demand fair treatment or challenge discriminatory practices. This complacency allows gender disparities to persist and even worsen. Only by confronting misogyny can women collectively push for the changes needed to achieve true gender equality.

Sometimes the world feels more hostile to women than ever. But reading through the stories gathered here, I feel hopeful rather than downbeat. And I'm intrigued when Mary tells me that despite everything – the rise of malign influencers like Andrew Tate; the growing toxicity of Twitter/X under its new owner Elon Musk; the fact that Trump has won a second term – she thinks public discourse is, on the whole, less misogynistic than it used to be. 'I think it's got better, and when things get better it often happens in fits and starts . . . When the zeitgeist changes it's not that people act differently all the time, it's that reactions to them change . . . We're never going to be in a kind of nirvana in which everything is as we'd like it to be.'

I hope that in the course of reading this book you've found practical strategies as well as helpful insights. Remember that climbing the ladder is not a solitary journey: it requires a collective effort from individuals, communities and societies. Men must be allies. Employers must create inclusive workplaces where women are encouraged to excel and take on leadership roles. Educational institutions should promote self-confidence among girls from an early age, not least because with self-confidence comes a self-knowledge that increases and become more beneficial as we get older.

Again, Mary puts this brilliantly. 'Being sure of yourself often goes together – it's the other side of the coin – with knowing your frailties and fragilities and where you're bad and don't live up to your ideals. This is a terribly old-fashioned virtue and people I've taught recently would think it really marked me as a 1970s feminist, but I think gaining a bit of thick skin and resilience is an extremely useful thing. I totally accept that we should live in a world where you don't need to be resilient. But a bit of not caring [is important] and I suppose it takes you several decades. When the business with AA Gill and co happened, my daughter said, "You wouldn't be so confident about this if you were thirty years younger."'

Female empowerment isn't just a moral imperative. It's a practical necessity for the betterment of society as a whole.

For all women, a ladder awaits. Just remember to enjoy the view when you've reached the top.

NOTES

1 https://www.unwomen.org/en/news/stories/2020/11/state
   ment-ed-phumzile-international-day-for-the-elimination-of-
   violence-against-women.

2 Kate Figes, *Because of Her Sex: The Myth of Equality for
   Women in Britain* (Macmillan, 1994), p67.

3 Hilary M Lips, *Women Across Cultures* (CUP, 2021), p5.

4 The title of historian Jane Robinson's 2020 book about female
   pioneers, *Ladies Can't Climb Ladders*, refers to a story from
   the early 1900s: male members of the Royal Institute of British
   Architects, worried about the threat of female infiltration,
   apparently comforted themselves with this thought.

5 https://www.mckinsey.com/featured-insights/diversity-and-
   inclusion/women-in-the-workplace.

6 https://www.statista.com/chart/20835/household-tasks-uk-
   by-gender/.

7 Interviewed by Ayesha Hazarika on Times Radio (1 May
   2022).

8 Leonard Mlodinow, *Elastic: Flexible Thinking in a
   Constantly Changing World* (Allen Lane, 2018), p6.

9 'Women working from home risk being caught in a
   "she-cession"', *Guardian* (12 November 2021).

10 Virginia Woolf, 'A Sketch of the Past', *Moments of Being*
   (Hogarth Press, 1976), p67.

11 Timothy D Wilson, *Redirect: Changing the Stories We Live By* (Penguin, 2013), ebook.

12 Geena Davis, *Dying of Politeness* (William Collins, 2022), p4.

13 Gloria Steinem, *My Life on the Road* (Oneworld, 2015).

14 Jean-Paul Sartre, *Being and Nothingness* (Simon & Schuster, 1992), p102.

15 Simone de Beauvoir, *Memoirs of a Dutiful Daughter* (Penguin, 2001), ebook.

16 ibid.

17 https://www.tuc.org.uk/news/2-5-bme-workers-experience-racism-work-new-tuc-report.

18 'Women of colour held back from senior roles by "structural racism"', *Financial Times* (30 August 2021).

19 Mikki Kendall, *Hood Feminism: Notes From the Women White Feminists Forgot* (Bloomsbury, 2020), ebook.

20 Parm Sandhu, *Black and Blue: One Woman's Story of Policing and Prejudice* (Atlantic, 2021), ebook.

21 Edith Wharton, *A Backward Glance* (Everyman, 1993), ebook.

22 Kjerstin Gruys, *Mirror, Mirror Off the Wall: How I Learned to Love My Body By Not Looking At It For A Year* (Avery, 2013), ebook.

23 Sonia A Krol and Jennifer A Bartz, 'The Self and Empathy: Lacking a Clear and Stable Sense of Self Undermines Empathy and Helping Behavior', *Emotion* 22(7) 1554–71.

24 Simon Baron-Cohen, *Zero Degrees of Empathy* (Penguin, 2012), ebook.

25 https://www.channel4.com/news/by/jon-snow/blogs/fine-play-crying-game.

26 'Reading literary fiction improves empathy, study finds,' *Guardian* (8 October 2013).

27 George Eliot, 'The Natural History of German Life', *Westminster Review* LXVI (July 1856), pp28–44.

28 Pauline R Clance and Suzanne A Imes (1978), 'The Imposter Phenomenon in High Achieving Women: Dynamics and Therapeutic Intervention', *Psychotherapy: Theory, Research & Practice, 15*(3), 241–47.

29 Sheryl Sandberg, *Lean In* (Ebury, 2013), p28.

30 https://www.paulineroseclance.com/impostor_phenomenon.
html.

31 Manfred FR Kets de Vries, *Reflections on Character and
Leadership* (Wiley, 2010), ebook.

32 Valerie Young, *The Secret Thoughts of Successful Women*
(Crown, 2011), p139.

33 ibid., p137.

34 Deborah Tannen, 'The Power of Talk: Who Gets Heard and
Why', *Harvard Business Review (September–October 1995)*.

35 Quoted in John Bank and Susan Vinnicombe, *Women With
Attitude: Lessons for Career Management* (Routledge,
2003), p247.

36 ibid., p42.

37 Roz Shafran, Sarah Egan and Tracey Wade, *Overcoming
Perfectionism* (Robinson, 2010), p15.

38 Rachel Gable, *The Hidden Curriculum: First Generation
Students at Legacy Universities* (Princeton University Press,
2022), p15.

39 Eileen Atkins, *Will She Do?: Act One of a Life on Stage*
(Virago, 2021), ebook.

40 Elizabeth Bowen, *A Time In Rome* (Vintage, 2003), ebook.

41 ibid.

42 Cyril Connolly, *Enemies of Promise* (University of Chicago
Press, 2008), p121.

43 https://www.mckinsey.com/featured-insights/diversity-and-
inclusion/women-in-the-workplace.

44 Clare Balding, *My Animals and Other Family* (Penguin,
2012), ebook.

45 Harriet Harman, *A Woman's Work* (Allen Lane, 2017),
p102.

46 ibid., p115.

47 Deirdre Beddoe, *Back to Home and Duty: Women Between
the Wars 1918–1939* (Pandora, 1989), p132.

48 Joanna Goldsworthy (Ed.), *A Certain Age: Reflecting on
the Menopause* (Virago, 1993), p5.

49 https://www.cipd.org/en/about/press-releases/menopause-at-
work/.

50 Julia Gillard and Ngozi Okonjo-Iweala, *Women and Leadership* (MIT Press, 2022), p11.

51 Kristi Gray and Dorislee Gilbert, 'Sexual Assault Prosecutions', *Hating Girls: An Intersectional Survey of Misogyny*, eds. Debra Meyers, Mary Sue Barnett (Brill, 202s1), p9.

52 Kate Manne, *Down Girl: The Logic of Misogyny* (Penguin, 2019), p102.

53 Sandy Doyle, *Trainwreck* (Melville House, 2016), ebook.

54 *Woman's Own* (31 December 1932).

55 Caroline Criado-Perez, *Invisible Women: Exposing Data Bias in a World Designed for Men* (Chatto & Windus, 2019), ebook.

56 Sandy Doyle, *Trainwreck* (Melville House, 2016), ebook.

57 Helena Kennedy, *Eve Was Framed* (Vintage, 2005), p12.

58 ibid., p6.

59 ibid., p9.

60 Mary Ann Sieghart, *The Authority Gap* (Transworld, 2021), ebook.

61 www.independent.co.uk/life-style/women-work-jobs-sexism-promotion-leadership-science-a8742531.html.

62 Joyce F Benenson (2013), 'The development of human female competition: allies and adversaries', *Philosophical Transactions of the Royal Society B: Biological Sciences*, 368(1631).

63 Julia Gillard and Ngozi Okonjo-Iweala, *Women and Leadership* (MIT Press, 2022), p227.

64 Tsedale M Melaku and Christoph Winkler, 'How Women Can Identify Male Allies in the Workplace', *Harvard Business Review* (4 May 2022).

65 Interview with Sue Crockford from 2012, www.bl.uk/sisterhood/articles/womens-liberation-a-national-movement.

66 https://www.forbes.com/sites/sianbeilock/2020/01/07/how-to-address-subtle-friendly-sexism-at-work/.

67 Alice Farnham, *In Good Hands: The Making of a Modern Conductor* (Faber, 2023), ebook.

68 ibid.

69 Brenda Hale, *Spider Woman* (Bodley Head, 2021), ebook.

70 Tanni Grey-Thompson, *Seize the Day* (Hodder & Stoughton, 2001), ebook.

71 Clair Wills, *Lovers and Strangers: An Immigrant History of Post-War Britain* (Penguin, 2017), ebook.

72 Nimko Ali, *What We're Told Not To Talk About (But We're Going To Anyway)* (Viking, 2019), p12.

73 Marie-Christine Heinze, *Yemen and the Search for Stability* (Bloomsbury, 2018), pp50–51.

74 Arthur Miller, *Timebends* (Methuen, 1987), p4.

75 https://www.oxfordmartin.ox.ac.uk/blog/how-immigration-has-changed-the-world-for-the-better/.

76 https://hbr.org/2018/10/research-shows-immigrants-help-businesses-grow-heres-why.

77 Joan Didion, *The Year of Magical Thinking* (Harper Perennial, 2006), p3.

78 ibid., p10.

79 ibid., p225.

80 Susan Jeffers, *Embracing Uncertainty* (Hodder & Stoughton, 2017), ebook.

81 'Human insight remains essential to beat the bias of algorithms', *Financial Times* (4 December 2019).

82 https://www.internationalwomensday.com/Missions/14458/Gender-and-AI-Addressing-bias-in-artificial-intelligence.

ACKNOWLEDGEMENTS

First and foremost, I want to thank all the women featured in *The Ladder* for giving me permission to include their stories and quote from their interviews. Thank you also to:

My colleagues at Times Radio, especially Tim Levell, programme director, for giving me the space and encouragement to come up with the concept; Sandra Glab, executive producer, for her talent, dedication and friendship; Aletha Adu and Melissa Tutesigensi-Charles, who did so much in the early days to bring in great Ladder guests; and my current producer Emily Leahy, whose calm determination and indefatigability has seen the show go from strength to strength.

Esme Wren, Anna Hughes and all the Channel 4 News family. Arabella Pike, my wonderful, ever-exacting editor at William Collins, and her team.

My literary agent Antony Topping at Greene & Heaton. My TV agent Helen Purvis, for helping me hone the original concept.

And finally, the biggest thank you to my wonderful husband John – who helped out editorially as the deadline loomed – and our patient, always-supportive daughters Scarlett and Molly. They encouraged me up every rung of my own ladder.